"*10 Great Dates: Connecting Faith, Love & Marriage* goes beyond spending time together. It offers guidance on deepening an emotional and spiritual bond. Each exercise addresses present-day relational struggles and stressors by providing insight and opportunities to authentically know and be known in new ways, bringing honor to one another and glory to God."

—Gayle DiMartino, marriage ministry director,
Willow Creek Community Church

"This book is both practical and fun. It gives couples tangible ways to grow together spiritually all in the fun, guilt-free format of great dates. The Larsons and Arps have done the work. All you need to do is carve out time for your 10 Great Dates!"

—Gary Smalley, author of *The DNA of Relationships*

"Don't settle for an individual faith walk when connecting spiritually as a couple could transform your marriage. This book provides an effective road map for couples who want to journey together."

—Drs. Les and Leslie Parrott, #1 *New York Times*
authors of *The Good Fight*

"Isn't marriage supposed to point us to God and teach us to be more like Christ, and if so, how do you strengthen your soul and build the soul of your marriage at the same time? This wonderfully written book takes what often is an elusive and mysterious discipline for couples and provides 10 life-building opportunities to move past the mundane of life and get to what really matters. Experience it!"

—Ron L. Deal, author of *The Smart Stepfamily*
and coauthor of *The Remarriage Checkup*

"Few things possess the potential to add to the overall satisfaction and meaning of marriage like really connecting spiritually. The Larsons and the Arps do an amazing job of gracefully and playfully helping us walk together toward fulfilling our deepest longings and desires."

—Robert Paul, co-president, National Institute of Marriage

"After years of writing, teaching and encouraging couples, one common question I'm still asked is, 'How do I connect with my spouse on a spiritual level?' Finally, here is a book that helps couples do just that, and all in the fun format of Great Dates. I highly recommend this book for couples, small groups, and churches who want to strengthen and build godly marriages."

—Gary Chapman, PhD, author of *The 5 Love Languages*

"With its focus on spiritual intimacy, this book is a refreshing change from the standard marriage materials on emotional and physical connection. The Larsons and Arps have provided us with an amazing resource filled with fun and creative ways to help us develop our spiritual connection."

—Shawn Stoever, PhD, senior director, WinShape Foundation

"This book will refresh your marriage. You can't beat the life-changing content, 10 meaningful dates, and the wisdom of some of America's finest marriage experts. Our goal is to personally connect deeper over the next three months with each of these dates."

—Jim and Cathy Burns, authors of *Closer: 52 Devotions to Draw Couples Together*; speakers at Creating an Intimate Marriage seminars

"Being intentional in any relationship is key to its success. Peter and Heather and David and Claudia help couples see the importance of Date Night. This is a great resource for any couple."

—Tim Popadic, president, DateNightWorks.com

"God in your marriage . . . is everything. He brings new life, love, closeness, and hope every day. But while connecting with God together would seem so natural and easy to do, it isn't. I think that it matters so much to a healthy relationship that all hell is against it. Here's a fresh start to a new 'God life' together.

—Dr. Tim Clinton, president, American Association of Christian Counselors; executive director, Center for Counseling & Family Studies, Liberty University

"In working with hundreds of couples, the *desire* to build a strong, growing faith together as a couple is there—what hasn't been is what this book shows, how to get there! My friends David and Claudia Arp and Peter and Heather Larson use their proven, fun, easy-to-grasp Great Dates strategy to help you as a couple gain the greatest closeness possible—with your God. Great Dates can help you love a great God and your spouse even more!"

—John Trent, Ph.D., author of *The Blessing*; president, StrongFamilies.com

10 GREAT D♥TES

Connecting Faith, Love & Marriage

Peter & Heather
LARSON

AND

David & Claudia
ARP

BETHANY HOUSE PUBLISHERS
a division of Baker Publishing Group
Minneapolis, Minnesota

Published by Bethany House Publishers
11400 Hampshire Avenue South
Bloomington, Minnesota 55438
www.bethanyhouse.com

Bethany House Publishers is a division of
Baker Publishing Group, Grand Rapids, Michigan

Printed in the United States of America

Library of Congress Cataloging-in-Publication Data
Larson, Peter.
    10 great dates : connecting faith, love & marriage / Peter and Heather Larson & David and Claudia Arp.
        pages cm
    Includes bibliographical references.
    Summary: "Marriage experts provide ten date ideas to help married Christian couples connect spiritually and grow in their faith. Each date presents a different spiritual theme and includes suggestions for before, during, and after the date"—Provided by publisher.
        ISBN 978-0-7642-1134-8 (pbk. : alk. paper)
    1. Marital dating—Religious aspects. 2. Love. 3. Marriage—Religious aspects. I. Title. II. Title: Ten great dates.
HQ801.8.L37 2013
306.81—dc23   2013014949

The names and identifying details of individuals in the stories within have been changed to protect their privacy.

Cover design by Thinkpen Design

Authors are represented by WordServe Literary Group

13   14   15   16   17   18   19   7   6   5   4   3   2   1

This book is written to create a legacy
of spiritual growth in marriages,
starting with our own families,
children, and grandchildren.

May God richly bless your lives and your marriage.

Other Resources from David & Claudia Arp

10 Great Dates to Energize Your Marriage
(book/DVD curriculum)
10 Great Dates Before You Say "I Do" (book/DVD curriculum)
10 Great Dates for Empty Nesters
52 Fantastic Dates for You and Your Mate
The Second Half of Marriage (book/DVD curriculum)
Answering the 8 Cries of the Spirited Child
Empty Nesting (with Scott Stanley, Howard Markman,
and Susan Blumberg)
Loving Your Relatives
The Connected Family
Family Moments
Marriage Moments
No Time for Sex
Quiet Whispers from God's Heart for Couples
Suddenly They're 13!
PEP Groups for Parents (DVD curriculum)

Other Resources from Peter & Heather Larson

The Couple Checkup (with David H. Olson and Amy Olson-Sigg)
10 Great Dates Before You Say "I Do" (DVD curriculum)
PREPARE to Last (DVD curriculum with David
H. Olson and Jeff & Debbie McElroy)
PREPARE/ENRICH: Customized Version
(inventory/assessment with David H. Olson)
Couple Checkup (inventory/assessment with David H. Olson)

Contents

Welcome to Your Great Dates 9

Your Dating Plan 20

Your Dating Ground Rules 21

10 Great Dates

Date 1: Connecting Faith and Love 23

Date 2: Appreciating Your Differences 35

Date 3: Experiencing God Together 53

Date 4: Getting Into the Word 69

Date 5: Loving Your Closest Neighbor 83

Date 6: Talking Together With God 97

Date 7: Building Your Marriage on a Strong
           Foundation 113

Date 8: Facing the Storms of Life Together 131

Date 9: Guarding Your Hearts Under God's Canopy 143

Date 10: Making Your Marriage a Lighthouse 157

Contents

Acknowledgments   171

Notes   173

About the Authors   175

Exercises for Dates 1 to 10: Duplicate Copies for
  Each Spouse

Welcome to Your Great Dates

Welcome to your own 10 Great Dates. For years we've been helping couples build their relationship through the habit of dating. Now we're adding a new dimension to our Great Dates. We want to introduce you to 10 Great Dates especially crafted to help you connect faith, love, and marriage in ways that result in a deeper spiritual connection—all in the fun, guilt-free, safe format of Great Dates.

If you are feeling a bit apprehensive or skeptical, that's okay. We understand. Perhaps you have tried unsuccessfully to connect spiritually. If so, you are not alone. Others have had similar experiences. We encourage you to relax. You can trust us. This unique approach to growing together spiritually will help you find that deeper spiritual connection you are longing for, and it can even help you overcome the "it just doesn't work for us" syndrome.

"It Just Doesn't Work for Us!"

Whether young or old, newlywed or married thirty-plus years, religious or not, couples talk to us about their desire to experience spiritual intimacy, but many struggle with knowing how to integrate their faith with their marriage. We often hear comments like,

> *"We tried to grow together spiritually, but it just didn't work for us."*
>
> *"We know we should pray together, but it's just not easy to do."*
>
> *"We want to have devotions as a couple, but past attempts have resulted only in frustration and disappointment."*
>
> *"I want us to be closer to God, but how can I get my spouse to talk with me about our faith or other spiritual topics?"*
>
> *"Life is just too busy. We really don't have the time to connect spiritually. I leave for work before my wife gets up, and in the evening, I'm just too tired for deeper conversations about faith."*
>
> *"We'd definitely like to develop more spiritual intimacy, but we don't know where or how to start."*

Do you identify with any of these comments? Have you experienced similar frustrations? We have. We understand. Years ago, when God became real in our lives and we grew closer to our heavenly Father, we wanted to experience growing closer to each other spiritually, but our own efforts were unsuccessful. We tried. Oh, how we tried!

For instance, we (the Arps) knew we should be having devotions as a couple, so each January we made a resolution to take at least a few minutes each day to read through a yearlong devotional book together. We would start January 1, thinking, *This is the year we will really do it!* But by January 15, we were already a week behind. Before long, we stopped even trying. It was just easier to pursue growing spiritually individually than to try to have devotions as a couple.

We knew we should pray together, but one of us was more verbal than the other—not a good scenario for couple prayers.

Soon we joined the ranks of couples who also found it difficult to relate to each other in the spiritual realm.

We (the Larsons) came from families where spirituality was mainly an individual experience with God. We didn't have a model of what connecting spiritually with each other could look like. Our earliest attempts were only when we were desperate for God's help. Then it was more of an SOS for God to show up in our marriage.

If you can identify with our experiences, then these Great Dates are designed especially for you. It's time to give up the "we shoulds," let go of past disappointments, and join us on fun dates that can jump-start spiritual growth and put new excitement and energy into this very important aspect of your relationship.

All you need to do is to find a spot on your calendar for your ten dates. If ten dates sounds too daunting, another option is to do five dates, take a break, and then do five more. Find the plan that works best for you. Then relax and enjoy your dates. We've taken care of all the details and will be your guide on your couple spiritual pilgrimage.

Extend Grace From the Start

Most couples are at different places on their spiritual journeys, but it doesn't have to be stressful—if we're willing to accept diversity in the expression of our faith. A spiritual journey isn't stagnant; otherwise it's not a journey. Growing together spiritually gives you an opportunity to encourage each other in your faith. So for couples who are at different "scenic overlooks" in your spiritual pilgrimage, we offer the following suggestions as you begin your dates:

- *Don't force or coerce your spouse to attend or do something with you that you know he or she will not enjoy.* God does

11

not force us to do things against our will—so let him be your model.

- *Be teachable and willing to learn.* Whatever road you take, be willing to learn from others. Someday you may look back with amusement, acknowledging you were not as smart as you thought you were. With being teachable comes the need to grow and change, so watch out for closed-mindedness and rigidity. Be open for God's Spirit to teach, lead, guide, and enlighten you.

- *Realize that one of the privileges and joys of a marriage is only having to relate one-to-one.* You don't have to settle theological or denominational issues or settle disputes among countries or even factions in your church or group. A little diversity can spice up a relationship.

- *Be positive and patient.* God stands at the door and knocks. He waits like a gentleman for us to open the door. He doesn't bang it down. Likewise, we can invite our spouse to join us on this journey, pray for him or her to desire to grow together spiritually, and then be patient as we allow God to make the changes.

Your Dating Coaches

In the following pages we will be your date coaches. No matter where you are in life, married without kids, or with a full house like the Larsons, or empty nesters like the Arps, there is something here for every couple.

You'll find that these dates are fun, safe, and easy to do. If you've experienced any of our other 10 Great Dates, you have a head start. If not, don't worry, we've taken the work out of the dates and designed them so that wherever you are on your faith journey—even if you're at different places—you can start connecting together spiritually right away.

We want you to think about each date as a couple's devotional but without the pressure and obligation often associated with attempting to have devotions with your spouse. They are not intended to be guilt-producing. Instead, you will have the opportunity in a relaxed setting to move closer to each other and to God. Our dating topics are centered on spiritual concepts that can be applied to your marriage relationship. We'll help you look at biblical passages through a "marriage filter." For instance, when looking at the story of Jesus washing the disciples' feet, how would that relate to marriage? Maybe one of us needs to offer to wash the dishes after dinner tonight or look for other ways to choose humility and serve our spouse. With each date we'll also give a few easy-to-do devotional suggestions (that we refer to as Post-Date Spiritual Discovery times) for those who want to connect spiritually between dates.

Your 10 Great Dates

Now it's your turn. Although you are welcome to skip around from topic to topic, we have organized the chapters to build on one another. Diving in on praying together may be easier when you have taken the time to create a foundation of love and understanding of where each of you are on your spiritual journey. Here is a more detailed description of the topics ahead.

Date 1: Connecting Faith and Love

On this date, you'll talk about how connecting faith in your marriage can help you build a more loving, growing relationship. You'll share your own unique experiences that impact where you are today on your spiritual quest. Appreciating and understanding your past will help you forge a closer relationship in the future with each other and with God.

Date 2: Appreciating Your Differences

If you want to grow together spiritually, you will need to be able to appreciate and accept the ways you are different from each other. You must also be willing to forgive each other. No relationship has a greater potential for anger than the marriage relationship. How you manage your differences and disappointments with each other will affect your spiritual intimacy, so on this date you'll talk about two key core values: acceptance and forgiveness.

Date 3: Experiencing God Together

Where and when do you feel the closest to God? We are different and our differences influence where and how we worship and feel close to God. On this date, you'll talk about factors that bring you together spiritually as you worship God together.

Date 4: Getting Into the Word

Reading the Bible together can foster spiritual intimacy, but some couples find this experience rather threatening. If one is more of a pusher, and the other one more passive, it's easy to feel either coerced and manipulated or frustrated and dissatisfied. To get into the Word together will require making sure it is not a competitive experience. On this date, we will give you some simple tools to help you grow spiritually through studying the Bible together.

Date 5: Loving Your Closest Neighbor

So who is your closest neighbor? If you're married, it's your partner—the one you've chosen to share life with at its deepest and most intimate level! How are you doing with loving your partner? Are you able to give each other unconditional love during the hard times? Do you naturally look for and accentuate the positive? On this date, you'll talk about how to love and encourage your spouse.

Date 6: Talking Together With God

Praying together can be threatening and uncomfortable, but it doesn't have to be. Date 6 will help you see how prayer can promote spiritual closeness. You'll talk about how to overcome some of the obstacles to praying as a couple and practical ways to develop a meaningful prayer life together.

Date 7: Building Your Marriage on a Strong Foundation

In the beginning, God created marriage, and it was very good. In Genesis 2:24, he gave us three fundamental principles that help us have a strong foundation for our marriage. On this date, you'll talk about the importance of what the Bible calls leaving, cleaving, and becoming one.

Date 8: Facing the Storms of Life Together

Struggles in life will either pull you together or push you apart. Can you think of a hard time that you experienced as a couple that brought you closer together spiritually? This date will help you talk about how to stay close and face the storms of life together.

Date 9: Guarding Your Hearts Under God's Canopy

If you want to stay close spiritually, you need to guard your heart. There are over nine hundred verses in the Bible that contain the word *heart*, including Proverbs 4:43, which tells us to "guard our heart." In the Jewish wedding tradition, the canopy signifies God's protective covering for the bridal pair. On this date, you'll look at what it means to have God's sacred canopy over your marriage and how to guard your heart.

Date 10: Making Your Marriage a Lighthouse

In Genesis 1:26–27, we read that God created man male and female, in his image. It's amazing, but as a husband and wife we have the potential to reflect God's image—to be a lighthouse to marriages around us. Date 10 encourages you to talk about how you can continue to draw close spiritually and how your marriage can be a lighthouse to those around you.

Your Personal Dating Guide

Following each chapter is your own personal dating guide. We've taken care of the details so you can concentrate on connecting spiritually with each other. You will find a pre-date guide with suggestions for how to prepare for each date, ideas for where to go, how to approach each date, and how to benefit from the dating exercises, which are in the back of the book. We have provided duplicate copies of the exercises, and the pages are designed to make them easy to take on your date.

While it is desirable for both of you to read the corresponding chapter before the date and fill out the exercise, we realize sometimes this just won't happen. So with each Dating Guide we have included a brief chapter summary.

While our 10 Great Dates are designed to help one couple at a time, they are also appropriate for small-group studies. We have an easy-to-use leader's guide available at *www.10greatdates.org* as a free download. If you know you need the accountability of being committed to others, recruit other couples to join you on this faith adventure.

The Dating Format

So how do these dates work? It's quite simple. First, read the corresponding chapter before each date. If only one reads the chapter, that person can take the lead in planning the date and guiding the conversation.

Second, go on your date, bringing along your copies of that particular date's exercise. (Remember, the exercises are found in the back of the book.) In a relaxed atmosphere, away from interruptions, you will have the opportunity to talk through the short exercises that will help you grow closer spiritually. The practical application during the date in an atmosphere of fun is the secret of having great dates! Plus, we are hoping your date night will be a habit you will continue. You can reap the benefits of your Great Dates long past these initial ten.

Launching Your Great Dates

The following steps will help you begin your dating experience on a positive note.

1. Agree to go on these Great Dates. It really doesn't matter who found the book or whose idea it was, going on your ten dates will help you take a closer look at how you can develop spiritual intimacy.

2. Schedule your dates and get them on your calendar.

3. Have a strategy for possible interruptions. Despite the best planning, you may have to change your plans. When this happens, reschedule your date for the same week and persevere. Hang in there and value your time together. Don't let other things crowd out time for dating and focusing on each other.

4. Anticipate each date. Let the other know you are looking forward to being together. Be clever. Send text messages, leave sticky notes around, and give hints that you expect a great date.

5. Before the date, read through the chapter and note key topics to discuss. If you take time to complete the short

exercise before the date, you will have more time for intimate conversations. But you can also do the exercise on the date.

6. Follow our simple guide for each date and stay on topic. Don't use date time to deal with other issues and problems.

7. Stay positive! It's hard to be negative when you are holding hands.

8. Get started and have fun!

Make a Commitment

Our Great Dates will only make a difference if you do them. Like most anything worthwhile, building spiritual intimacy takes time. Good intentions aren't enough. A written commitment can help carry you through. Use the commitment form that follows to record your promise to each other.

You will be glad you took the time to connect faith and love in your marriage. Remember, yesterday is past, and tomorrow is in the future. Today is the only gift of time you've been given; that's why it's called "the present." So give each other the present of 10 Great Dates!

Making a Commitment

I agree to invest time in connecting spiritually by going on 10 Great Dates.

Officially Signed:

_____

_____

Date _____

Our first date is scheduled for _____

 # Your Dating Plan

Write in when you are going to have each date!

Date 1: Connecting Faith and Love
is scheduled for _____

Date 2: Appreciating Your Differences
is scheduled for _____

Date 3: Experiencing God Together
is scheduled for _____

Date 4: Getting Into the Word
is scheduled for _____

Date 5: Loving Your Closest Neighbor
is scheduled for _____

Date 6: Talking Together With God
is scheduled for _____

Date 7: Building Your Marriage on a Strong Foundation
is scheduled for _____

Date 8: Facing the Storms of Life Together
is scheduled for _____

Date 9: Guarding Your Hearts Under God's Canopy
is scheduled for _____

Date 10: Making Your Marriage a Lighthouse
is scheduled for _____

Your Dating Ground Rules

To get the most out of each date:

- *Read the corresponding chapter and/or chapter summary.* If you have not filled out the exercise, do so before you begin your discussion.

- *Stay positive!* This is not the time to tell your spouse what he or she has done wrong.

- *Be future-focused.* Focus on what you want your relationship to be like in the future. Don't concentrate on past failures. (It's okay to remember past successes.)

- *Talk about your relationship.* Do not talk about your job, children, or in-laws, unless it's part of the topic of the date.

- *Give a gift of love.* Some topics will interest you more than others. On the less exciting ones, give a gift of love: Participate enthusiastically!

- *Don't force it.* If you get on a negative track, stop that discussion. Move on to another topic you both feel good about.

- *If you get stuck, ask for help.* If during your dates an issue comes up that you can't handle together, talk to your pastor, mentor couple, or counselor.

- *Use good communication skills.* Be prepared for some surprises and new insights about each other. They can open new opportunities for growth and spiritual intimacy in your relationship. Following are tips for sharing your answers:

  1. Be honest, yet never unkind.
  2. Start your sentences with "I." Talking about yourself will help create an open environment where your spouse will feel safe and less defensive.

3. Resist attacking the other or defending yourself.

4. Be specific and positive.

- *Have fun!* Also, think about *why* you are dating. It is to enrich your relationship and grow together spiritually.

- *Between each date, do the suggested devotional either together or individually.* Remember: You are developing healthy habits that will enrich your life together long after your 10 Great Dates are completed.

1

Connecting Faith and Love

Let us not give up meeting together, as some are in the habit of doing, but let us encourage one another.

Hebrews 10:25 (NIV1984)

Welcome to Date 1. On this date, you will have the opportunity to consider the role faith plays in your life individually and as a couple. You may find that connecting spiritually will also bring you closer to each other in other areas of life. For instance, research suggests that spiritual intimacy can even benefit your love life! In a national sample of over 24,000 married couples who took the ENRICH inventory, those with a high level of spiritual agreement were two times more satisfied with their sexual relationship than couples with a low level of spiritual compatibility.[1]

Not only does current research show the benefits of a spiritual dimension in marriage, it's also evident in writings from ages past. Consider this description of a spiritually intimate marriage by Tertullian in the second century:

How beautiful is the marriage of two Christians, two who are one in hope, one in desire, one in the way of life they follow, one in the religion they practice. . . . Nothing divides them, either in flesh or in spirit. They pray together; instructing one another, encouraging one another, strengthening one another.[2]

While this is a beautiful picture of a spiritually intimate marriage, we have to admit that we're not quite to this point. In fact, we have a long way to go. Still, we want to share a bit of our journey with you in hopes that it will encourage you in your own spiritual pilgrimage.

Peter and Heather's Story

I (Peter) didn't even know we could or should embark on a journey of connecting together spiritually. Despite the fact that I was a graduate student in a seminary when we got married, I was focused on my psychology degree, and thought our relationship was fine just the way it was. We went to church most Sundays, prayed before meals, and both believed in God. This is why I was a bit confused and intimidated when Heather began suggesting we could do more.

In our first year of marriage, Heather told me she wanted to pray together on a regular basis. I nipped that idea in the bud. I calmly explained to my new wife that my prayer life and relationship with God was very personal. Wasn't it enough that we worshiped together on Sunday mornings? Looking back, I just wasn't ready for that level of vulnerability in my spiritual life.

Next, Heather suggested we get more involved with a small group through church. This too was an uphill battle. I was the classic example of a stealth church attendee, preferring to fly under the radar. Just a few smiles and head nods was all it took, and I could do my weekly appearance quickly and painlessly without wasting half my Sunday talking to people I barely knew.

This had always been my approach to church. Even though I grew up attending the church my parents took us to, I never felt a part of it and didn't connect with other kids in the youth group. I was used to attending church more as a requirement of Christian life, not because I really wanted to be there.

I (Heather), on the other hand, grew up very active in my church—from youth choir and service groups to summer camps. I spent half the week at church and enjoyed a variety of leadership roles too. I was comfortable praying and sharing devotions with others.

I assumed Peter would want to bring spiritual activities like prayer and devotions into our marriage. I remember his response when I suggested we pray together at night. I felt surprised at his lack of interest and hurt that he didn't want to connect with me spiritually the way I expected.

Dave and Claudia's Story

Our first attempts to connect spiritually didn't work out well either. We had been married for several years before we started on our faith journey together. We wanted God to help us be the best partners and parents we could be, but we weren't sure how to go about it. A bit of history.

I (Dave) began my spiritual journey in high school through the influence of my grandmother and a Sunday school teacher who explained to me how I could invite Jesus Christ into my life. As a teenager, I remember reading my Bible, and I was very involved in my youth group in my church. For my high school years, I had what I would describe as a close relationship with God. Then when I went to college, I put my Bible on a shelf and began to drift away from God. It wasn't until several years later,

25

after we were married and after the birth of our first baby, that I began to remember my spiritual heritage and became interested again in growing in my faith.

I (Claudia) grew up in the church and loved God, but I didn't know much about Jesus. It wasn't until after our first son was born that I understood who Jesus Christ was and his significance in my faith journey. We were living in Atlanta when Martie, a good friend from college days, asked me to go to a women's Bible study with her. I was fascinated with the ladies I met and the things I heard as I kept attending this class. Before long, I began to understand how much God loved me and what an amazing gift he provided through his Son, Jesus. Wow! Did my life change! Of course, I wanted to share my newfound faith with Dave, whom I assumed was not a Christian. I won't give you the details, but this was not a pretty time in our marriage.

Dave Remembers

When Claudia became a Christian, her newfound "spirituality" made me uncomfortable. I saw her life changing but didn't appreciate her subtle and not-so-subtle attempts to get me on board spiritually. I'd done that in high school, and I resented her insinuations that I wasn't a Christian. But through a couple of business friends who reached out to me, I came to the point of rededicating my life to Christ. So that should have been the time we would get it together spiritually as a couple, right? Wrong!

Claudia Remembers

Our relationship did improve, but we didn't know the first thing about how to travel this spiritual journey together. We got involved in a church and had several friends who kept inviting us to a couple's small-group Bible study. I was dying to go, while

Dave was doing everything not to go. He later told me he felt I knew more about all of this than he did, which made the idea of talking about God with other couples to be very threatening. I was persistent, though, and finally he agreed to go.

I was thrilled! I knew if I could just get Dave to the group, he would love it and we would be on our way to growing together in our faith. I loved that evening's study, especially sitting there with my husband. For me, it was similar to the women's Bible study I attended, and I couldn't wait to get home and hear how much Dave liked it. Instead, I remember him saying, "Claudia, some people need this sort of thing. I don't! So don't ever ask me to go to something like this again."

I was crushed. *How could he not like it?* I was disappointed in him—and in God. In retrospect, it wasn't that Dave and I didn't want to connect spiritually—we just didn't know how to jump-start it. Forcing him to do it my way definitely wasn't the answer!

Years later, as we look back on our faith journey together, we wish we had had the wisdom to take a different path—one in which we would have given each other the grace to grow at our own individual pace. I wish I had not felt obligated to continually take Dave's "spiritual temperature" and instead simply trusted God to work in his life. He didn't need me to be his own private "holy spirit" to nudge him along the path.

What's Your Story?

After talking with many couples, we know our stories are not unique. Unfortunately, what often happens after an unsuccessful attempt (like our Bible study experience) is that couples stop trying to connect on a spiritual level. Their relationship with Christ becomes compartmentalized as a "private matter." Sure, they may attend church together and serve others and support

Christian endeavors together, but they don't truly relate to each other on a spiritual level. They may even pray together occasionally, but over time they settle in at a safe distance and have less than a spiritually intimate relationship.

Your Spiritual Memory Lanes

On your first date, we want you to look back at your own spiritual journeys and share them with each other. If we had done this early on, we might have bypassed some misunderstandings and hard times!

Think about your earliest awareness of God. Did you grow up in a churchgoing family? Were your parents Christians? Did you trust Christ as a child, or were you an adult when you understood how to become a Christian? If one of you grew up in a Christian home and the other became a Christian as an adult, you each have a unique perspective of God's love and grace to share with each other. Or if you aren't sure where you are on your journey, consider these dates as a wonderful opportunity to learn more about God and how spiritual intimacy can bring you closer together as a couple. If you aren't at the same place spiritually, it will benefit your relationship if you are able to better understand your partner's thoughts and beliefs.

How do your unique experiences and personality reflect where you are today on your spiritual quest? For instance, even though I (Dave) had been a Christian since high school, I never participated in a small-group Bible study. That first one with Claudia made me so uncomfortable. Even today I'm not a "groupie." More recently, when we moved to Virginia, it took us three years to join a small-group study, mainly because of my resistance. But this time Claudia didn't push me. She waited until I was ready. Then we started praying we would find a group where we would fit. One Sunday after church we ran into a friend who is on staff at our church and asked her if she knew a group that we might relate to well. She made a couple of phone calls, and before we knew it, God had answered our prayer.

Any new situation can cause apprehension, but this time we *both* wanted to go and take that step of faith together. And how glad we are that we did! We both enjoy our small-group Bible study, but it's because we chose it together. We both feel safe in the group because we have gotten to know and have built trust with the other couples. What if one of us had not felt comfortable? If one was uncomfortable, we would have kept looking for a group. We had agreed that either of us had veto power, so we could both feel safe in trying it out.

We share our more current experience with you for a few reasons. First, to let you know we can change. I (Claudia) am no longer Dave's "holy spirit," and Dave doesn't automatically resist my suggestions as a knee-jerk reaction. Together, we recognize our unique differences and how they play out in the spiritual realm. While I may be the one who feels the greater need for being in a small group, Dave is the one who is more sensitive to the needs of others and is often the motivator in giving to others. His generous spirit and attitude encourages me to give even when I would naturally resist initiating this type of outreach.

We too (the Larsons) have come a long way since we first began our spiritual journey. After nearly twenty years of marriage and three children, I (Peter) am much more open to participating in a small group, openly discussing my faith, and even praying together with Heather. I've come to understand my initial resistance as a basic fear of being that vulnerable and intimate with my wife. For me, it took a combination of time, maturity, and God's leading in my life to understand the powerful benefits of connecting our faith in our marriage. I'm thankful that Heather didn't pressure or push me too hard in the beginning. Instead, she patiently and prayerfully brought her request to God and let him work in my life. You'll hear more about this process in the upcoming dates!

Appreciating Your Past—Anticipating Your Future

We hope you're getting our point. Different isn't negative. Growing together spiritually is not a competition. Our experiences are different. We don't have to be at the same place on our individual journeys, but we do want to journey together. So we hope that on this first date you will enjoy getting to know each other a bit better as you share your spiritual journeys together and talk about your future path!

Now it's time for your first Great Date! Use the following simple dating guide and enjoy your trip down your own spiritual memory lanes and celebrate connecting your faith, your love, and your marriage.

Great Date 1

Connecting Faith and Love

Date 1 will help you understand your spiritual journey and identify where you are today and how you want to travel on this spiritual pathway as a couple.

Pre-Date Preparation

- Read chapter 1, "Connecting Faith and Love."
- Find your copy of the Date 1 Exercise (in the back of the book) and make any notes you like. Looking over the exercise before your date gives time for reflection. Also, if one of you is more verbal than the other, writing out some notes will give you time to formulate your thoughts.
- Make reservations at a favorite restaurant. The one making the reservations may want to let the place be a surprise.
- Think about what you will wear. Dress in a way you think the other will like. Remember, this is a date!

Date-Night Tips

- Plan to use the whole evening.
- During a leisurely dinner, talk through the questions in the Date 1 Exercise.
- Enjoy talking about your individual spiritual journeys— where you are today and how you want to continue your journey together as a couple. (Don't worry if you don't get all the way through the exercises. Your conversation can be continued at another time.)

Chapter Summary

Each of our spiritual journeys up to this point is just that, a journey, with ups and downs. This may be your first step in starting a spiritual journey together, or you may have made some attempts in the past. The Larsons each had different expectations of how their spiritual life should look in marriage. Heather wanted to be open and active in her spiritual life, while Peter was looking for a more personal and private experience. The Arps' spiritual journey began with a bit of a tug-of-war. Claudia was excited about her new faith, and she wanted Dave to have the same enthusiasm she did. Dave resisted her attempts to join small groups where he would have to be more open about his spiritual journey. Years later, both couples share that their relationships have grown to a new level of intimacy and love as a result of connecting faith and love in their marriage.

Now you will have a chance to reflect on your spiritual journeys. Appreciating and understanding your past will help you forge a closer relationship in the future with each other and with God. You can build a more loving relationship as you share your own unique experiences that have an impact on where you are today on your spiritual quest. One caution: Growing together spiritually is not a competition. Our experiences will be different. We don't have to be at the same place on our individual journeys, but we would like to journey together. So we hope that on this first date you will enjoy getting to know each other a bit better as you share your spiritual journeys together and talk about your future path!

Post-Date Spiritual Discovery

Connecting Faith and Love

Sometime after each date, we suggest a spiritual discovery time together. Try to set aside about fifteen minutes of uninterrupted time when you can seek the Lord as a couple. If you are not feeling ready to do this devotion as a couple, you can try it individually. Here is a suggested guide, or you can choose one from your favorite devotional book or another source.

1. Pray—Open with a simple prayer such as:

   God, we invite you to lead us on our faith journey together. We commit ourselves to you and to each other as we seek your truth in our lives.

2. Read—Genesis 1:26–31

3. Discuss—It's a wonderful mystery to us, but somehow when we build our marriage based on his Word and live out the principles Jesus taught, we have the potential to reflect God's image to others. Wow! That blows us away. However, we have to admit that often we fall short of reflecting his image to others even though the potential is there!

   • How is marriage a reflection of God's image?

   • How might your marriage change this week if you embraced the truth that God is the author of your marriage and has pronounced it "good"?

4. Apply—Read Psalm 34:3 and list some ways you can glorify God together this week.

5. Close in prayer—Thank God for your time together and ask your spouse how you can be praying for him/her this week.

2

Appreciating Your Differences

Be kind and compassionate to one another, forgiving each other, just as in Christ God forgave you.

Ephesians 4:32

To connect spiritually in your marriage, you need to appreciate and accept the ways you are different from each other. This has not always been easy for us to do. Accepting our differences involves two biblical core values: acceptance and forgiveness. How well we are able to accept and forgive each other will affect how much spiritual intimacy we will have in our relationship together and with God.

Did you ever notice that the traits that attracted you to your spouse *before* marriage can become irritating *after* marriage? Before we were married, I (Claudia) just loved how easygoing and laid-back Dave was. He was never in a hurry and had all the time in the world to listen to me.

Claudia liked to talk and I (Dave) liked to listen. From the start I was attracted to her energy and enthusiasm for life. She was always in motion, and it was never boring being around her.

Then we got married. Claudia's endless lists of places to go, things to do, and people to see tired me out. All I wanted were quiet evenings at home, which was boring for Claudia.

The first few years of marriage, we managed to do some compromising. However, in the back of our minds, we usually wanted *the other* to do the changing. Claudia's perspective was "If Dave were more like me and a bit more motivated, we'd get along better." And me? I wanted Claudia to slow down and not take life so seriously. Even when we were new in our faith and really trying to develop spiritual intimacy together, we still struggled with accepting each other as we were.

Accepting Each Other

Fast-forward a few years to when we joined the staff of a Christian organization. One of the first things we had to do was take a battery of psychological tests. Our differences were obvious even in the way we filled out the questionnaires. Claudia labored over each question and cross-checked her answers for consistency. I quickly answered the questions while watching a football game on television. What we didn't know was that the next week we would sit down with the staff psychologist and discuss the results.

We were not surprised when he told us how different we were. But he didn't stop there. He pointed out that my strengths were Claudia's weaknesses and vice versa. And then he gave us a great challenge: If you work together and let each person operate in his or her area of strength, you can be a wonderful team together.

We wish we could tell you we immediately went out and applied this new information to our relationship. It took time.

It's not easy to admit your spouse is better in an area than you are. It was awkward at first to try to change how we handled various areas of responsibility, but we kept trying, and over the years we have seen the benefits. Once we began to concentrate on our strengths, we began to accept each other with all our strengths and weaknesses. The same is true for our spiritual life. We have different spiritual gifts, and when we appreciate each other's spiritual gifts, we are able to accept where each is on his or her individual spiritual pilgrimage as well as on our pilgrimage together.

On this date you'll have the opportunity to talk about how you are alike and how you are different. You will affirm your individual strengths and talk about how they benefit your marriage relationship. You will also talk about your spiritual giftedness. In 1 Corinthians 12:4–5, we read that God has given each of us unique spiritual gifts, all of which are valuable. Maybe you have never thought much about your own spiritual gifts, but identifying your gifts (strengths) and accepting your partner's will foster spiritual intimacy.

For Heather and me (Peter), Heather clearly is gifted in the area of hospitality. She loves to prepare an amazing meal, make our home feel warm and inviting, and serve friends and family by hosting a brunch or dinner. She's the first to offer to drop off a meal to a sick friend or acquaintance. And as the only daughter among her siblings, she's quick to volunteer to host family holidays at our home. Combine this gift with her outgoing personality, and there is always the potential for a party or event showing up on our calendar.

I do not share this gift, but I've tried to understand and accept Heather's desire to extend hospitality to others. It used to be that I resented her constant busyness and drive to serve others. I felt it robbed me of needed downtime and sometimes put a dent in our monthly budget, as it can be expensive to host a dinner or holiday gathering. After learning and talking more about her personality and gifts, I now know it brings her true joy and blesses those she touches with her hospitality. She uses that same gift as a wife and mother to make each day special in our home. We've now found ways to compromise and make sure we balance outward expressions of hospitality with time and resources for our own family as well. For me, acknowledging her gift of hospitality as a gift from God helps me understand and value this difference in our approach to life.

In a recent study of 50,000 married couples who took the ENRICH Inventory, 52 percent of couples reported some disagreement about their spiritual beliefs. But when we compared the couples with the highest marital satisfaction to those with the lowest, the happy couples were 30 percent more likely to report that spiritual differences did not cause tension in their relationship.[1] In other words, spiritual differences are quite common, but happy couples are much more likely to accept their differences without letting them spoil the quality of their relationship. They extend grace to one another, and perhaps realize that neither of them is the sole authority on spiritual truth. That belongs to Christ.

With the many ways spouses differ from each other, it should come as no surprise that our spiritual lives will also be unique. Consider for a moment how you are two different genders with two very different personalities, coming from two different family backgrounds, each with their own traditions. Now add to this the fact that you likely grew up with two different experiences of church and faith. Is it any wonder you're bound to have your own set of expectations for what growing together spiritually will look like?

One way that Peter and I (Heather) are different spiritually is in the ways we prefer to worship. After growing up very involved in church, I find corporate worship an important part of my spiritual experience. My social personality allows me to enjoy meeting other believers each week. I also look forward to singing hymns or worship songs with others, receiving formal teaching, and praying with others. Peter, on the other hand, is more introverted and prefers meeting in a home with a small group of people to share in an informal style of worship. We have learned to honor and accept both of these styles of worship in our marriage rather than trying to change each other.

Forgiving Each Other

Closely related to acceptance is the core value of forgiveness. Without forgiveness we cannot build an intimate relationship with our partner or with God. We begin our spiritual pilgrimage through experiencing God's forgiveness and acknowledging the sacrifice Jesus made for us by dying in our place on the cross. Forgiveness is at the heart of the Christian faith, and in every healthy and growing marriage, couples willingly forgive each other. No one is perfect, and we often let each other down. Show us a marriage without forgiveness and we'll show you a marriage with bitterness, disappointment, and unresolved conflict—a marriage void of spiritual intimacy.

Realizing that Christ has paid our debt and forgives us for our shortcomings should motivate us to do the same for our spouse. When a long-term marriage crumbles, it's usually not the result of a major crisis or a one-time event. More likely it's the result of little things that have built up over the years. We need to forgive each other daily. To let go and forgive injustices, hurts, and disappointments will help you build a healthy Christian marriage.

Peggy is married to Greg, who is not the easiest person to live with. He is domineering, negative, critical, hard-driving, and demanding. Most people would have given up long ago, but not Peggy. We asked her to tell us her secret. "I never put a limit on forgiveness," she said. "I can't control Greg, but I can control me. I had to stop asking myself, 'What do I deserve?' And instead ask, 'What can I give?' I've always tried to grab the best from the past and focus on the future. Because my marriage is so precious to me, I choose to give Greg a clean slate each morning. I just throw away the hurts from the previous day, forgive him, and start over."

"And what about Greg?" we asked her.

"Over the years he has modified his behavior a little bit," she said. "For instance, he is beginning to spend less time at work and more time with me!"

This type of grace flies in the face of what our world teaches today. But so does Christ's teaching when asked by his disciples how many times we should forgive another who sins against us. Perhaps Peter thought he was estimating high when he suggested seven times, but Jesus answered, "Not seven times, but seventy-seven times" (Matthew 18:22).

Clearing the Slate

Take a couple of moments and think about your relationship with your spouse. Do you need to give your partner a clean slate? If forgiveness is so vital, how do we handle all the daily irritations and from time to time the larger issues that divide us? How can we really accept each other's quirks and shortcomings? We suggest the following exercise. This is not a couple's exercise or one that you should do on your date. If you need to forgive your spouse, take some time alone to go through the following steps:[2]

1. *Identify grievances.* Okay, here's the list you may have rattled off in your head, or to your spouse, a thousand times—you know, all those things you'd like to change

about your spouse. Now write them down! You won't show this list to your spouse (you'll shred, burn, or bury it when you're through), but you need to articulate to yourself once and for all that you're letting go of these little grievances that have been such big irritations. Do it now!

2. *Evaluate grievances.* Now take this list and evaluate:

   • Which issues can be easily forgiven and forgotten or accepted (like leaving unwashed dishes in the kitchen sink)?

   • Which issues need some special closure because they still cause you some pain (your partner's refusal to take up your favorite activity)?

   • Which issues need to be discussed because you need to find a way to move forward together (like agreeing on how you're going to manage your finances when one is a saver and the other a spender)?

   • Which issues will take a serious effort on your part, perhaps even professional intervention, to overcome (affairs, no lovemaking, abuse, destructive communication patterns)?

3. *Decide to forgive.* For each item on your list, ask yourself if you are willing to forgive your spouse and let go of this issue between you. Remember, forgiveness begins with a simple decision, a simple act of the will. We are to forgive as God has forgiven us. It is not dependent upon our spouse asking for our forgiveness or even acknowledging he or she has done anything wrong.

4. *Let go.* With your categorized list, decide on an appropriate send-off for the easily forgiven and accepted irritations. Perhaps setting this list on fire and dropping it into the toilet will help you let go. For the very serious hurts and disappointments, we recommend seeking some professional help, especially if there are times you have felt unsafe because of someone's temper or found their anger intimidating. If you've already worked through your

pain and disappointment, take pride in how far you've journeyed toward improving your relationship. Surviving marital strife with your relationship intact can only increase your potential for a loving, fulfilling marriage.

5. *Change your responses.* Now that you have forgiven your spouse, how will you respond to these issues in the future? The next time you sense irritation rising, try to turn the situation around by replacing your negative thoughts with something more positive.

Replace the Negative

When we camp on what our spouse is doing wrong, it's easy to get in the habit of negative thinking. Physician Daniel Amen, author of *Change Your Brain, Change Your Life*, writes about how negative thinking can actually adversely affect our body and relationships. He explains that we all have *automatic negative thoughts*, which he calls *ants*, but it's what we do with those thoughts, or ants, that makes a difference.[3]

Dr. Amen encourages us to talk back to the ants. He gives the illustration of how our negative thoughts can easily multiply. If you're at a picnic, one or two ants might be irritating, but a whole army of ants can ruin your party. If you don't take care of the ant problem in the beginning, you can forget the picnic. We've observed that it only takes one or two negative thoughts to start us down a negative path, where we focus on what's wrong rather than on what's right. So here is Dr. Amen's suggestion: When you have a negative thought, write it down, and then write down a more balanced response to that thought. For example,

Ant: "My spouse never listens to me."

Your new response: "He didn't talk to me when I wanted him to. He was busy with something else, but he often talks with me. I just got him at a bad time."

Ant: "She's not interested in making love with me. Guess I'm just not desirable to her."

Your new response: "She was tired tonight and not in the mood, but when she's more rested she's a great lover and we're good together!"

The principle of replacing the negative with the positive is biblical. The apostle Paul gives this advice:

Finally, brothers and sisters, whatever is true, whatever is noble, whatever is right, whatever is pure, whatever is lovely, whatever is admirable—if anything is excellent or praiseworthy—think about such things.

Philippians 4:8

If Paul can write this while he's in prison and believe it in his heart, we can certainly practice this principle in our marriage. Why not make your own Philippians Positive List? It will help you wipe out the ants and focus on what's great about your partner. A great way to do this is to secretly look for at least one positive thing your partner does or says each day. If you're stuck in the rut of negative thinking, it may be hard to recognize the positives right away. So when you notice one, write it down so your list begins to grow. Furthermore, compliment your partner when you catch him or her doing something positive. At first, this might seem strange for both of you, but you'll soon find you're spending more time paying attention to the positives and less time dwelling on the negatives.

Once we get on a more positive path, we may realize that most of the time, our reaction to our partner's perceived shortcoming is probably worse than whatever our partner did or did not do, and that we may be the one who needs to ask for forgiveness. While we try to accept each other's little irritating habits, we also need to look at our inappropriate reactions and follow Jesus' admonition not to look at the speck in someone else's eye until we take out the log in our own (Matthew 7:3). Often we are so concerned with our spouse's different perspective that we cannot see our own inappropriate reaction. To help you focus on your own part, we suggest going through the following steps of "log removal."

Getting Rid of the Log

Step One: Look over your previous list of what irritates you about your spouse and then consider your inappropriate responses. On a sheet of paper, make two columns. In the left column, list your spouse's behaviors that trigger a reaction in you. In the right column, list your inappropriate responses to those grievances. Perhaps your spouse spends considerable time checking email and text messages. Do you assume automatically he or she doesn't care or is trying to ignore you by focusing attention elsewhere? What is your response? Do you lecture, sigh, criticize, get even, or give the silent treatment?

You may find that your responses are worse than your spouse's behavior. If so, admit your negative attitude and burn or tear up the paper. Do not show it to your spouse; this exercise is for your benefit to help you get the log out of your own eye! The following example may help.

Differences in my spouse that trigger my reaction:	My inappropriate responses:
Example: Distracted by email and text messages	1. Belittle
	2. Nag
	3. Compare with others
	4. Criticize
	5. Neglect
	6. Reject
	7. Be cool sexually
	8. Get angry—blow up
	9. Give the silent treatment

Step Two: Focus your attention on your inappropriate responses and attitudes. We must learn to take responsibility for our own actions and reactions before we can work on our relationships with others. Besides, the only thing we can really control is our own actions/reactions. You can have the quickest and most powerful effect on your relationship when you take responsibility for yourself.

Step Three: Accept your spouse with his or her strengths and weaknesses. Are you thankful for your spouse's strengths and weaknesses? Remember: Your spouse's temperament can complement your own. It is impossible to change another person; we can only change ourselves. But when we concentrate on correcting our inappropriate responses and attitudes, wonderful things often happen. Others change in response to us. So don't waste time trying to change your spouse. Concentrate on being the person your partner needs.

Step Four: Ask your spouse's forgiveness for your past inappropriate responses. No relationship can thrive without forgiveness. No marriage is perfect; we all blow it from time to time. Relationships are like potted plants. The pot can be broken, but if the plant is repotted, if it is watered and given tender loving care, it will continue to grow and thrive. Forgiveness is a vital part of marriage. Without it, relationships die—like the potted plant left with its roots exposed. If your spouse asks you for forgiveness, give it. The director of a mental-health facility once said that half of his patients would be able to go home if they could forgive and knew they were forgiven.

How to Say You're Sorry

If you need to ask for forgiveness, focus on what you have done wrong—"I was wrong to nag you about checking your messages.

Will you forgive me?"—*not* on your spouse's shortcomings: "I'm sorry I nagged you about checking your email, but you know it's wrong to always let this distract you!" Remember, you are pointing a finger at *your* inappropriate response. Don't use this moment as an opportunity to attack your spouse. If you attack your partner, you're attacking your own marriage team.

A word of caution: Let us repeat! If you find you need to go through the process of Log Removal, do not share your list with your spouse. This exercise is a private one, just for you, to get the log out of your own eye!

Get Back on Track

Connecting together in your walk of faith cannot continue when there is a spirit of resentment or unforgiveness in your relationship. Faith and love will grow when you are able to see your spouse's strengths and appreciate your differences. Do you see ways your differences complement each other and give balance to your team? Together you can discover ways to compensate for areas in which you may be too much alike. Appreciate the uniqueness of your marriage relationship. You can use your differences and your unique spiritual gifts to grow closer spiritually to each other and to God.

Now it's time to enjoy Date 2. Follow this Dating Guide and get ready to appreciate your differences and celebrate your spiritual gifts!

Great Date 2

Appreciating Your Differences

Date 2 will give you the opportunity to consider how you can benefit from each other's spiritual strengths and how you can complement each other in the ways you are different.

Pre-Date Preparation

- Read chapter 2, "Appreciating Your Differences."
- Preview the Date 2 Exercise (in the back of the book).
- Plan to go to your favorite hangout.
- Choose a place where you can talk privately.

Date-Night Tips

- While discussing this chapter's topics, concentrate on your partner's spiritual strengths and affirm the ways your differences can complement each other.
- If you are at different places on your spiritual journey, be sensitive to each other.
- Talk about what you have in common.
- This is an opportunity to share your inner feelings. It is not a time to try to change your partner.

Chapter Summary

Do you remember what first attracted you to your spouse? It may be that he was outgoing or that she was relaxed. Now those qualities may be the very things that get under your skin. Before moving forward together spiritually, it is important to recognize our differences. Identifying our differences may not be the hard part, but accepting them and not trying to change our spouse can be more difficult. Most likely, your spouse also has different spiritual gifts from the ones you have. Maybe you have never thought much about spiritual gifts, but identifying your gifts (strengths) and accepting your partner's gifts will foster spiritual intimacy and allow you and your spouse to flourish.

Part of accepting each other's differences is being able to forgive each other. To clean the slate, sometimes we need to take a look at the lenses we are wearing. They may need cleaning. If we are looking for the negative in our spouse, we are sure to find it. How do you respond when your spouse does something that irritates you? Your response may be perpetuating the problem! Saying you're sorry and asking for forgiveness isn't easy, but it's the first step in moving toward creating a marriage that can grow deep spiritually. For more on forgiveness in your marriage, refer to the specific steps outlined in this chapter. How you manage your differences and disappointments with each other will affect your spiritual intimacy, so on this date you'll talk about two core values: acceptance and forgiveness.

Post-Date Spiritual Discovery

Appreciating Your Differences

Have a brief devotional time together before your next date. Try to set aside about fifteen minutes of uninterrupted time where you can seek the Lord as a couple. If you are not feeling ready to have this devotional time as a couple, you can try it individually. Below is a suggested devotional exercise, or you can choose one from your favorite devotional book or another source.

Celebrate Your Differences

1. Pray—Invite God to be present in this time together and to give each of you a heart of acceptance and forgiveness. You can use this simple prayer:

   Lord, we ask you to be present with us. May we each be willing to forgive one another in response to your immeasurable forgiveness of us. Give us eyes to see how we can accept and appreciate each other's differences.

2. Read—1 Corinthians 12:12–31 and Romans 12:3–13

3. Discuss—When you identify and appreciate your God-given differences and spiritual gifts, you can gain a better understanding of your marriage relationship, accept each other, and build on your strengths. Your goal should be to build a strong marriage by benefiting from each other's strengths and appreciating each other's differences.

   • Why do you think Paul linked his teaching about gifts with a comparison to the body?

- How do Paul's words, written for the early church, relate to your marriage?

- Notice in both passages how the discussion of gifts and the body flow into powerful messages about love.

4. Apply—Find a way you can love and appreciate your partner this week in spite of his or her differences.

5. Close in prayer—Thank God for your time together and ask your partner how you can be praying for him or her this week.

Bonus Devotional: Discover Your Spiritual Gifts

God gives each believer a spiritual gift to use to serve him and others. Each gift is important in furthering God's kingdom. This brief exercise is designed to help you identify your spiritual gifts. Read Romans 12:1–8. Below are a number of spiritual gifts and a brief description of each. Check one or more categories that best describes how you see yourself helping others.

____ Serving: demonstrating love by meeting practical needs

____ Teaching: speaking to others with emphasis on searching out and validating truth

____ Mercy: identifying and comforting those in distress

____ Exhortation: to come alongside someone with words of encouragement, comfort, consolation, and counsel to help them be all God wants them to be

____ Giving: sharing personal assets to further the ministry of another

___ Administration: to steer the body toward the accomplishment of God-given goals and directives by planning, organizing, and supervising others

More spiritual gifts are mentioned elsewhere in the Bible. If you feel that your gift is not on this list or if you want to explore this topic more, several spiritual gift assessments are found online, including

www.spiritualgiftstest.com

www.ministrymatters.com/spiritualgifts

http://mintools.com/spiritual-gifts-test.htm

These are a few sites that are helpful, but there are many others. You may consider getting life-coaching in this area or a program such as LifeKeys[4] to help you understand more about the gifts God has given you to be used in his service.

3

Experiencing God Together

A cord of three strands is not quickly broken.

Ecclesiastes 4:12

On Date 2, we talked about how accepting each other's differences enriches and promotes spiritual intimacy. Another way to connect spiritually in your marriage is to experience God together. Where do you feel close to God and naturally desire to praise and worship him? For us, it's when we're out in the middle of God's creation.

One of our (the Arps') favorite great dates is hiking in the mountains. When we're leading conferences close to mountain ranges, we sometimes tack on a few days to hike and get refreshed. High up on a mountain trail is one of the places where we feel closest to each other and to God. Over the years our hikes have progressed from easy walks around lakes and in forests to more strenuous hikes high up above the tree line.

We both enjoy hiking, but sometimes we have differing opinions of which trail to take. Dave is usually the more adventuresome, and I am the more cautious one, but one time I pushed the limits. It was a beautiful autumn afternoon, even though rain clouds were threatening and nightfall was only a few hours away.

On this brisk afternoon, we hiked for about two hours on a pleasant path by the edge of a rushing stream that climbed up from the valley below. Hiking is where we often pray together, and we had a wonderful time with each other and the Lord thanking him for his blessings and lifting up current needs. The afternoon slipped by, and before we realized it, it was time to turn back. Here is one of our differences. Dave never wants to turn around, and will go to great lengths to find an alternate way back. I am usually the one keeping up with the time and insisting we turn around and safely go back the way we came. But on this day, at the turning-around point, we came to a fork in the road. I first noticed the sign indicating a road back to the town where we had parked our car was only one and a half hours away. If we took this high road we would get back before dark with a few minutes to spare. So, surprising Dave, I suggested that we take that route back to our car.

Dave, shocked that I was so adventuresome, immediately agreed, so off we went climbing the "high road" back. What a beautiful walk it turned out to be! Snaking higher and higher around the mountain, we could see the valley below. We even came across a little snow and ice, but the breathtaking scenery—the beauty of God's creation—was worth it.

Now, the high way up should eventually wind down to the village, right? An hour passed and we were still climbing higher and higher. And it was getting later and later, and the clouds were getting darker and darker. At last we could see the little village below, but the road kept going up and up. We came to a red sign pointing to town—but it wasn't on a road. It was on a steep path to what appeared to be a sheer drop-off. Surely this wasn't the way back. We went on for a few more minutes on the road, but it just kept going higher and higher and daylight was running out. At that point, I wished we had gone back the way we came, but it was too late to try to retrace our way back.

Not wanting to spend a cold, rainy night on the mountain under a starless sky, we backtracked to the steep path and agreed that, as treacherous as it looked, it was the only way down. Fortunately, we had our hiking poles, so together we began the most tedious and nerve-racking hike of our lives. The path twisted through dark forests heavy with roots and across ski trails, over fences, and through what seemed to be a path leading nowhere. Finally, we came into a clearing—actually, it was a steep pasture complete with cows—but down below we could see the lights of the town where we had parked our car. The rain was now more than a drizzle, but slowly, cautiously, we made our way down to our car. Soaking wet but safely in our car, our fear turned to pride that we had conquered such a difficult trail. We both felt God had sent his angels to guide us safely back to our vehicle.

We love telling our family (and all who will listen) about our "high road" adventure. It was also a spiritual experience; we did a lot of praying on the way down! While we may prefer different pathways in the mountains, together we experienced a hike we will never forget. And on that day, we felt close to each other and close to God. Nature does that to us. It's easy to worship when we're looking at nature. Outside is where we both feel God's presence the most.

Where Do You Feel Close to God?

Where do you naturally feel the presence of God? Your answers might be different, but we find that our differences enhance our spiritual life. Our friends Todd and Jennifer prefer different worship styles. Todd grew up loving going to church. He resonated with the ritual, and even if the pastor was not so inspiring, he felt close to God just being in the church. In the same setting Jennifer was bored. She wanted to "feel" God. The fact that "God is there" didn't satisfy the longing in her heart. Over the years, Todd and Jennifer have looked for compromises when it came to choosing churches. Both enjoy hiking and biking together and, like us, also feel close to God when they are out in nature.

Jason and Morgan told us of a recent experience where they went on a weekend discipline of silence. Through solitude and simplicity they drew close to and worshiped God. Another couple we know loves activities that involve service and caring for others. Others can feel close to God when studying the Bible.

Gary Thomas, in his excellent book *Sacred Pathways*, challenges readers to discover their own sacred pathways. Gary writes, "A sacred pathway describes the way we relate to God and how we draw near to him. Do we have just one pathway? Not necessarily. Most of us, however, will naturally have a predisposition for relating to God, which is our predominant spiritual temperament."[1]

Think about your own spiritual life. Where and when do you feel the closest to God? Where do you worship with abandon? What about your spouse? Do you see ways you might be different in your approach to loving God? Can you think of times in the past when you have experienced God together?

We (Peter and Heather) recently sat down to brainstorm times we've experienced God together. Like many couples, we've had some of our most powerful experiential moments out in nature, when we've come face-to-face with God's awesome creation. As a newlywed couple living in California, we frequented Yosemite National Park for hikes and camping trips. One of our favorite memories of Yosemite happened over an Easter weekend camping trip with two other couples. One of the couples was Jewish and offered to take us through a traditional Seder dinner, commemorating the Jewish Passover. It was fascinating to learn more about this important tradition observed by Jews through-out history, including Jesus himself. Sitting outside by a campfire in a Yosemite mountain valley only added to the experience. As the evening wore on, the sky clouded over and a light cold rain began to fall. Filled with good food and appreciation for this new experience, we retired to our tents for the night.

The next morning, we awoke to a glorious sight. The clouds had cleared, the sun was up, and a brilliant blue sky outlined the peaks surrounding the valley. During the night, the tempera-ture had dropped and the light rain turned to snow, which now covered everything in a white blanket, reflecting the brilliance of the morning sun. Together, we walked alongside a stream through the rapidly melting snow to an outdoor Easter morning chapel service. Worshiping together with snowy mountains and glimpses of distant waterfalls surrounding us was a powerful experience of being in the presence of God.

While mountains and nature can make it easier to experience God together, we also have the opportunity to experience God as we move through the routines of everyday life. Peter and I have found that a key to experiencing God is putting him at the center of our lives, embracing an awareness of his presence in every aspect of our lives.

I choose to believe in a worldview that places God as our sovereign creator who loves us all. This view allows me to see the many shades of green in the trees as an expression of God's love for his creation. A near-miss accident is an opportunity to see how God is my protector. An unexpected bonus is seen as God's provision for me. Even difficult people in my life are easier to be around when I remember that God loves them, created them, and even died for them! This pathway to experiencing

God does not have to depend on an external setting or situation, but relies on an internal acknowledgment of God being actively present in our daily lives. With this in mind, you may be surprised by how often God creeps into your consciousness.

Any experience, large or small, positive or negative, can lead to an acknowledgment of God at work in your life: the birth of a child, planting a garden, enjoying a meal, listening to a great sermon, watching your children grow up, singing praise and worship songs, or even walking through a trial together. If we are paying attention, we can experience God in all things, allowing him to inform our decisions, reactions, relationships, and priorities.

Developing Spiritual Intimacy As a Couple

Experiencing God together helps develop spiritual intimacy. When we talk about spiritual intimacy, we think of emotional closeness with God. And our experience has been that emotional closeness with God contributes to emotional closeness and spiritual intimacy with each other. While spiritual intimacy defies a simple definition, to us it has two main components that are easier to understand: spiritual discovery and identifying core beliefs.

Spiritual Discovery

First is the commitment to spiritual discovery—to loving and worshiping God together and acknowledging his presence in every aspect of our lives. There are many ways couples can embark on a journey of spiritual discovery. For some, it will involve traditional approaches such as prayer, sacraments, Bible study, and worship. Others will experience God in creation as they hike mountains, sail seas, or sit by campfires under starlit skies. Some couples come to experience God during major events or transitions in life; a wedding ceremony, a birth, a graduation, or even challenges such as unemployment or death allow them the space to experience God's presence in their lives.

Remember, spiritual discovery doesn't have to happen alone. As a newlywed couple just moved to Southern California, Heather and I began to visit several churches, looking for a place we could worship. As we transitioned to regular attendees at one small congregation, we were invited to join a small group with other young married couples. I was skeptical and resistant about making this type of commitment. Who were the other people in this group? When did they meet? How long would it take? What would we have to do? Heather was excited about the opportunity. In the end, I agreed to try it and was blown away by what happened. As we got to know five other couples through a weekly gathering and invested in each other's lives, I began to appreciate our church on a whole new level. For the first time, I felt really connected at church. We formed lifelong friendships and together experienced God at work in our lives and marriages.

Drs. Les and Leslie Parrott affirm the importance of the spiritual dimension of marriage in their book *Saving Your Marriage Before It Starts*. They write, "The spiritual dimension of marriage is a practical source of food for marital growth and health. No single factor does more to cultivate oneness and a meaningful sense of purpose in marriage than a shared commitment to spiritual discovery. It is the ultimate hunger of our souls."[2]

Identifying Core Beliefs

The second component of spiritual intimacy comes as you define and understand your shared core beliefs, allowing those beliefs to be lived out in your relationship.

Think about your own core beliefs. What do you believe about life, death, God, marriage, family, and so on? Do your core beliefs encompass a relationship with God? What do you believe about Jesus and his teaching? What difference does this make in your daily life? If someone looked at your life today, what would they say are your core beliefs? Are you living them out day by day, or is your faith in God a "Sunday thing"? Where are you on your spiritual journey?

In the study of 50,000 married couples who took the ENRICH Inventory, the happier couples were more than twice as likely as unhappy couples (85 percent versus 40 percent) to report satisfaction with how they expressed and lived out their spiritual values and beliefs. Moreover, 78 percent of the happy couples reported feeling closer to their spouses because of their shared spiritual beliefs, while only 43 percent of the unhappy couples shared that sentiment. This research suggests that shared core beliefs lived out in the lives of couples is related to a higher marital satisfaction and a more connected relationship.[3]

Our Own Spiritual Journey

As we (the Arps) shared earlier, it was when Dave renewed his commitment to the Lord and I became a Christian that we began our spiritual journey together and started to examine our own core beliefs. Let us fill in some of the details of how we came to this point in our lives.

In the first years of our marriage, we had a great relationship even though we had little interest in the spiritual dimension of life. Relating to each other was easy for us. We were secure in our love. Sure, we had the occasional disagreement, but we didn't experience any serious stress until our first son was born. Then reality hit.

I remember the moment our first child was born as if it were yesterday. I waited to hear that first wonderful gasp for air and cry. Instead, silence—just the doctors and nurses rushing around.

Then I heard whispers. *What was happening? Was my baby in trouble? Would he live?* In my fear and panic, I cried out to God: "Please let my baby live!" In a few minutes, a loud cry became the first real answer to prayer that I can remember and defined the beginning of my spiritual search.

Married four years before having a baby, we were used to our freedom and flexibility. Both came to an abrupt end when our first child arrived. Not only were our wings clipped, but we were totally exhausted. We had never really understood the meaning of the little word *colic*. We got a quick education and had the bloodshot eyes to prove it. Also, since our baby had difficulty breathing at birth, we continually looked for signs of distress. (Our baby was normal—it was his parents who were distressed!)

For the first time, we began to snap at each other. We weren't getting off to a good start as partners in parenting, and I wasn't finding any spiritual answers. It seemed the harder we tried, the worse things got.

During this time, we were trying our best to stay connected. Long conversations brought us to the same basic conclusion: We were committed to each other and to our son, we had worked at developing intimacy in our relationship, but we needed more—we needed spiritual intimacy. We just didn't know how to find it.

Fast-forward a few years. We had moved to Atlanta, and now we were expecting our second child. It was during this time that I became a Christian and Dave started trusting the Lord again with his life. Our encounters with Jesus Christ at that point changed our lives forever. As God began to be more real to us in our own personal lives, we began to experience spiritual intimacy and closeness in our marriage. It was as if we had been plugged in to a new power source. Finding our security and significance in our relationship with Christ freed us to love and accept each other in a deeper way.

We realized that by growing closer to God, we could grow closer to each other.

Are you committed to pursuing a deeper faith connection in your marriage? On this date, you will have the opportunity to talk about your core beliefs. Drs. Les and Leslie Parrott affirm the importance of searching for shared beliefs, when they write: "Sharing life's ultimate meaning with another person is the spiritual call of soul mates, and every couple must answer that call or risk a stunted, under-developed marriage."[4]

Thousands of years ago, King Solomon saw the value of spiritual intimacy:

> Two are better than one, because they have a good return for their labor:
> If either of them falls down, one can help the other up.
> But pity anyone who falls and has no one to help them up.
> Also, if two lie down together, they will keep warm.
> But how can one keep warm alone?
> Though one may be overpowered, two can defend themselves.
>
> Ecclesiastes 4:9–12

Our relationship works best when we acknowledge our marriage cord has three strands. What are those three strands? Dave is one strand. I am another. And the third strand is God, the Holy Spirit. We see our marriage as a partnership with each other and a partnership with God. For instance, when we let each other down, we look to the third strand to keep our cord strong—to hold us together when our individual strands are frayed. It is God's forgiveness that empowers our ability to forgive each other. The third strand also helps us hang in there and get turned around even during times of discouragement.

Maybe you have faced crisis situations—an illness, financial stress, or a broken relationship. Whatever fears and problems you have faced or are presently facing, crisis times are times when extra resources are needed. These are the times you need to affirm those things that are truly important in life, and shared spiritual values will provide a welcome foundation.

We have shared with you our spiritual journey. Where are you in your journey? How is your faith connected to your core beliefs? What are your spiritual pathways? Where is the meeting place where you feel spiritually connected with your spouse? On this date, you're going to talk about it, so relax and enjoy affirming your own spiritual pathway.

Great Date 3

Experiencing God Together

Date 3 will give you the opportunity to talk about your core beliefs and factors that bring you together spiritually as you worship God together.

Pre-Date Preparation

- Read chapter 3, "Experiencing God Together."
- Preview the Date 3 Exercise (in the back of the book).
- Choose a location that will allow you to talk quietly— perhaps a picnic in a park or a bookstore with a coffee shop.

Date-Night Tips

- Discuss your exercise, alternating who goes first.
- Be prepared for some new insights into your spouse.
- Review communication tips in Dating Ground Rules, chapter 1.

Chapter Summary

Where do you feel close to God? For many, it is experiencing God in his amazing creation. We shared stories of experiencing God in nature while hiking or camping. Is it in church, when you're gathered with other believers? Others experience God in worship, solitude, studying the Bible, and through prayer. Experiencing God's presence together will help you grow spiritually intimate with each other. Commit to looking for ways to experience God together. You may want to try new things together. You may discover a new closeness to God as you serve meals to the homeless or celebrate a spiritual holiday in a new way.

Our core beliefs affect the way we live our lives. What do you believe about life, death, God, marriage, and family? What are your beliefs about forgiveness, hope, or pain in the world? Happier couples report feeling closer to each other because of their shared spiritual values and the way they are lived out together. The Bible tells us that a cord of three strands is not quickly broken (Ecclesiastes 4:9–12). When God is the third strand in a marriage, it has the strength to withstand trials, whereas a marriage built on human strength could easily break.

Post-Date Spiritual Discovery

Experiencing God Together

1. Pray—Open with a prayer, inviting God to draw near, such as:

   God, we ask you to draw near to us now as we seek your holy presence in our lives and marriage. Help us quiet our hearts that we may hear you and recognize you even in the busyness of our daily routines.

2. Read—Psalm 148. Now compare that passage to 1 Kings 19:11–13.

3. Discuss—Sometimes we experience God in the majestic presence of his creation. Psalm 148 beseeches all creation to praise the Lord: the moon, stars, sun, skies, mountains, hills, creatures, seas, and even the storms. In 1 Kings, however, Elijah doesn't find the Lord in the wind, earthquake, or fire, but in a gentle whisper passing by.

   • Is there a right or wrong way to experience God?

   • When have you seen God's presence revealed in powerful and majestic ways?

   • When have you felt his quiet, gentle whisper?

4. Apply—How can you be open and prepared to experience God together this week?

_____

_____

_____

_____

5. Close in prayer—Thank God for his awesome creation, which only begins to reflect his majesty. And thank him for revealing himself to you in the quiet, gentle whispers as well.

4

Getting Into the Word

Fix these words of mine in your hearts and minds; tie them
as symbols on your hands and bind them on your foreheads.
Teach them to your children, talking about them when you sit
at home and when you walk along the road, when you lie down
and when you get up. Write them on the doorframes of your
houses and on your gates.

Deuteronomy 11:18–20

Be careful what you pray for. God just may answer your prayers!
Years ago I (Claudia) remember praying that God would work
in Dave's life—that Dave would be transformed and follow God
all the days of his life. I wasn't prepared for the ways in which
my prayer would be answered. Fast-forward several years.

We were still living in Atlanta. The couple's Bible study Dave
had resisted was now a part of our weekly schedule, and we were
connecting more in our walk of faith together. We were both
studying and trying to apply God's Word to our lives. We now
had two young sons, a house and a mortgage, good Christian

friends, and a great church, and we were quite settled in life—or so I thought. Then one evening Dave dropped the bombshell. He had quit his job!

I was totally unprepared for this news. *How could he do this without discussing it with me?* As he told me the scenario of events, I tried to understand. I knew he was unhappy in the present position in the company, and especially with his heavy travel schedule, but I was not aware of how he was praying about it. He had prayed that if he was supposed to stay with this company, God would open the door for him to move to another division and position that would better suit his talents and not require so much time on the road away from his family. So when that didn't work out, he assumed God was leading him to quit his job. I was incredulous! Shocked! But as I saw how he was trusting God in this, I became more supportive. As I said before, be careful how you pray. God was answering my prayer, but not exactly as I wanted him to answer it.

This initiated a special time in our spiritual adventure to-gether. In a matter of a few months, Dave accepted a new job, but when the parameters changed and he realized he would be required to travel extensively in this job as well, he again quit. Then the real shocker: He announced that he felt God was lead-ing us to join the staff of a Christian ministry, Campus Crusade for Christ (CCC, now Cru). I wanted him to be excited about the Lord, but not to this extreme. What followed was an incredible adventure that led us to live in Germany and Austria for almost ten years, and eventually led to what we are doing today to help churches, communities, and couples build strong marriages.

A wonderful part of our time on the staff of CCC was the strong emphasis on studying God's Word. Before we moved to Europe with CCC, we would pack up our boys and drive cross-country to California for the summer to attend the In-stitute of Biblical Studies (IBS). What a rich time that was for us. We remember taking a course on Bible study methods with Josh McDowell, and sitting with Dr. Howard Hendricks as he taught us what the Bible says about building strong marriages and families.

It was wonderful to attend IBS together and take the same courses, but we also realized we were on our own individual paths. An important part of the process of listening to God speak was listening to God speak to us individually through our own personal Bible study and quiet times. We were looking for a balance of time in God's Word as individuals and together. To be honest, however, one of the most daunting challenges we have faced as a Christian couple is having quiet times with God together as a couple. This may seem like an oxymoron! How can you have a quiet time together? Once you begin to talk, you aren't quiet anymore!

For years we were dissatisfied with our couple devotional life, and frankly felt unsuccessful. Trying to arrange a specific time when we would be spiritually attuned to God *and* to each other was difficult. As we shared earlier, we started with high expectations, then we would miss a couple of times, get discouraged, and give up.

Also, if one of us was the driver and pusher and the other the more passive one, we found that devotional times together did not work. The passive partner felt coerced and manipulated, and the one pushing was frustrated and dissatisfied. So what is the secret? How can couple devotions be meaningful and promote spiritual closeness with each other and with God? We hope this new concept of Great Dates will help introduce a new paradigm for couple devotions.

Separate and Together

After trying unsuccessfully to have a quiet time together, we finally began to realize that truly meaningful couple devotions would only grow out of our own individual walks and quiet times with the Lord. In other words, the basis for couple devotions is to first meet individually with God and study his Word. Once we are filled and spiritually energized, we have something to share with each other.

Our friend Adrian shared the following story with us. It had been a very hectic, stressful week for his wife, Emma, and she was simply exhausted both physically and spiritually. Emma was scurrying around trying to get their three sons ready for church. As Adrian watched Emma, he realized how spent she was and said, "Emma, I want to take the boys to church today by myself, and I want you to stay home and rest."

Surprised at his suggestion—after all, isn't church where we go to get spiritually refreshed?—Emma knew she really did need some time alone, so she quickly thanked him.

Adrian told us, "I knew if Emma had time alone, she would be able to read the Bible and pray and that God would restore her spirit. And that's just what happened. When the boys and I returned home from church, I could sense that she had been spiritually refreshed. That afternoon, we had a very special time together when we talked about what God was doing in our lives, our marriage, and our family. That conversation would probably not have happened without Emma having had some time to restore her own soul through her own downtime with God."

Another option for couples with kids is to consider a family devotional time. Although this is not, strictly speaking, a couple time, it may be one way for both to be in God's Word in a significant way. One family we know discusses a Bible passage together each night at dinner. Significant life lessons and family values can be communicated in this way.

We (the Larsons) have needed to adjust our expectations and approach to getting into the Word as our marriage and family have developed. As newlyweds without children, it was much easier to carve out time for devotions and Bible reading as a couple. For the first several years of our marriage, Peter was a graduate student and had a very flexible schedule. I was a fifth-grade teacher with summers off. This flexibility, combined with thought-provoking content from many of Peter's summer theology classes, allowed us to read and discuss God's Word on a regular basis. We often integrated what Peter was studying into our spiritual journey as a couple. When he took courses on the Old or New Testament, we spent time discussing these scriptural passages and what he was learning from various professors. When he took a class on theology in films, we watched and discussed movies together. We read classic devotional passages from Christian writers and thinkers, and we even experimented with spiritual disciplines, such as fasting together. In our third year of marriage, we decided to each read the entire Bible in a year. We found a printed schedule that outlined how to read a section of the Old Testament, New Testament, and a Psalm each day. It was a rich time in our spiritual journey as a couple.

Almost twenty years and three children later, things are not so simple. Peter, now a licensed psychologist, works full-time and frequently has to travel to conferences and training events around the country. He is often up and out of the house early, usually before the kids are up. I get up early to have a personal Bible study, and then have "breakfast devotions" with the kids. My days are filled with shuttling our three children from one activity to another, volunteering in their classrooms, working with coaching clients, and writing blogs and books. As the kids grow, they seem to get busier with church, camps, sports, friends, and school activities. Add to this that we are increasingly being asked to coach, speak, and lead classes, and life has become exceedingly hectic.

It is unrealistic for us, in our current life-stage, to expect the same kind of time and flexibility we once had for studying

God's Word together. We are even noticing a shift in the type of small-group opportunities we pursue. It used to work best for us to participate in a small group together with other couples. But in recent years, as we try to balance the schedules of five family members, it has become easier for me to meet with other women for Bible studies during weekday mornings. Peter, on the other hand, meets on Wednesday nights with a group of guys for his Bible study. This divide-and-conquer approach also limits the number of baby-sitters we need each week.

Being flexible with one another allows each of us to pursue God's Word in fellowship with others while also attending to the responsibilities of parenting our three young children. Despite having our own Bible study groups, we try to check in with each other during our weekly date night to discuss what we are learning and what God is teaching us. A weekly time of couple devotions, like those outlined in this book, are a more realistic goal for many busy couples. As our children get older, we fully expect to re-engage in regular Bible study as a couple, but for now, we are being intentional about staying in the Word as individuals and getting fed on our spiritual journeys.

Our latest attempt to get into God's Word together has been to do just that. Read God's Word! As a New Year's resolution, we began reading a couple's devotional book together each night as we went to bed. We found we didn't relate well to the book, but we really enjoyed this time to connect before retiring each night. We decided to go right to God's Word and to take turns reading aloud and discussing a small passage together each night.

Tips for Getting Into the Word

Find a regular time. Whether you're going to dive into the Bible as a couple or each pursue an individual time of studying God's Word, we suggest you begin to make it part of your daily and weekly routine. Just as God gave the Israelites fresh manna in the desert each day, God gives us his Word each morning. Jesus reminds us that we cannot live by bread alone. It is God's Word that gives us the right nourishment for daily living.

Join a group. Joining a small group or weekly Bible study is an effective way to begin, plus it provides you with the direction and accountability of others going through the same experience. Many small groups will agree to read and study certain passages during the week as individuals, and then meet together as a group to discuss and apply the topics further. Take a course together. In our (the Arps') church you can take a series of courses called Christianity 101 to 501. Each course deals with a different aspect of living the Christian life.

Choose where to start. For many who have not studied the Bible, it can be a bit overwhelming to open to Genesis 1:1 and just begin reading from start to end. While this may work for some, we suggest beginning with the action-packed gospel of Mark. Follow up this book with Romans and Paul's letters in the New Testament. There are thirty-one chapters in the book of Proverbs, providing a rich resource of wisdom for each day of the month. Some find it helpful to set a goal of reading through the Bible in a year, and there are many outlines that break down a schedule of daily readings that cover the entire text.

There are organizations and Bible studies whose aim is to help people read, study, and apply God's Word in a meaningful way. Bible Study Fellowship (BSF) and Community Bible Study (CBS) offer courses all over the world. You can find a class near you via their websites: www.bsfinternational.org and www.community biblestudy.org. In addition, Precept Ministries offers a systematic way to study the Bible and many resources to help you form your own small group. See their website, www.precept.org.

If a group is not for you, you can find a Bible with commentary or application that will be relevant to you. You may even choose the *NIV Couples' Devotional Bible,* or something similar. Helpful resources on how to study the Bible are also available at www.scripturesalive.org.

With technology, you can use an online Bible or Bible app with suggestions for devotions and journaling. A great app that can help you start a Bible reading plan is YouVersion (www .youversion.com). It has several studies to choose from that will help you read and apply Scripture, including studies designed especially for couples.

To get started, ask four questions. Reading the Bible without knowing how to apply what you read can be discouraging and feel more like a task or a to-do list rather than a relevant activity. My dad (Heather's) taught me this simple four-step method years ago. He likes to joke that even though he isn't a morning person, he hasn't died yet from getting up an extra twenty or thirty minutes early! After reading a paragraph from Scripture, or just a few verses if the paragraph is too long, ask these four questions:

1. What does the passage say? You can look at this as a reporter would, answering the who, what, when, where, and why questions, or write out the few verses verbatim.
2. What does the passage mean? This is where you put what it means in your own words.
3. What does this passage teach about God? Look for God's character and attributes.
4. How do I apply this to myself? The Holy Spirit will help you see what God wants to communicate to you through this passage.

What I have found amazing is how the same passage can communicate something very different to me at different times in my life. You can finish with a simple prayer from your application questions.

Focus on God. So yes, "Seek ye first the kingdom of God . . ." is a good beginning to meaningful couple devotions. Once we both have met with God, we can then come together and share our spiritual insights with each other. But perhaps we should ask what it is we are seeking. Nurture for our souls? Striving to know God better? What is our focus when we read the Bible? A friend shared the following story on the importance of being God-focused when we study the Scriptures:

> One Sunday afternoon, I asked my children what they had learned that morning in Sunday school. They told me their teacher had taught them about the story of Jonah and how Jonah didn't want to go to Nineveh and he got in a boat going the other direction, but a big storm forced him out of the boat and he was swallowed by a big fish. They had all the details, but not once did they say they had learned anything about God—about the God of the storm, the God who loved Jonah, and the God who sent the fish to direct him to where God wanted him to be. This story is not only about Jonah but about our powerful God and how he cares for us and directs us even when we aren't going in the right direction. What are the fishes in your life? Where is God directing you to go? When we just focus on humanity (like my boys were just focusing on Jonah), we are not empowered spiritually.

Maybe we don't always focus on the "Jonah/humanity" side of the Scriptures, but maybe we too often put the focus on ourselves—*"What's in this passage for me?"* We see the Bible as a smorgasbord and concentrate on getting our own needs met. While it is true that God does meet our needs through his Word, how can we keep our focus on God and not just on ourselves? When studying a Bible passage, focus on what it tells you about God and what it reveals about your relationship to God.

Be creative. There are many options for getting into the Word these days. Take advantage of some of the new resources designed to give you quick and easy access to great scriptural teaching. Consider the following:

- Find a couple's devotional book you can relate to. One we (the Arps) especially like is *Closer* by Jim and Cathy Burns (Bethany House).
- Access an online daily devotional.
- Download an online sermon from a church website.
- Listen to the Bible online.
- Download a Bible app to your smartphone.

Now it's your time to take some of our suggestions and incorporate them into your lives. Get ready for a great date.

The following Dating Guide for Date 4 will help you explore ways to get "into the Word" both alone and as a couple.

Great Date 4

Date 4 will give you some simple tools to help you connect spiritually through studying the Bible together.

Pre-Date Preparation

- Read chapter 4, "Getting Into the Word."
- Complete the Date 4 Exercise (in the back of the book).
- Choose a location that will allow you to talk quietly— maybe a coffee shop or a library.

Date-Night Tips

- Be open to your spouse's suggestions.
- Look for commonality—where you both can feel comfortable studying the Bible together.

Remember, Bible study is not a competition!

Chapter Summary

Being on the same page spiritually is both important and challenging. While it is necessary to have a personal time of connecting with God through his Word, it can also be a great asset to your marriage to study the Bible together.

Studying the Bible as a couple can look different at different times in your life. You may find that the various stages of marriage allow for different types of study. Couples without children may find it easier to find time to study the Bible together, while those with young kids at home may need to be more creative. Be willing to be flexible.

This chapter offers several tips for getting into the Word. First, find a regular time when you can read the Bible together. Making it part of your daily or weekly routine will help you be nurtured by God's Word and truth. Also consider joining a small group or Bible study that will help provide accountability and give you new ideas for applying God's Word to your life.

Finding a reading plan or even choosing a place to begin can be difficult. Try one of the many online reading guides or simply read a Proverb a day to get started. When you read a passage and want to apply it to your life, try asking yourself four simple application questions. First, what does the passage say? Second, what does the passage mean? Third, what does it teach about God? And fourth, how do I apply this to myself? Remember to keep God the focus of your reading.

Post-Date Spiritual Discovery

Getting Into the Word

1. Pray—Open with a prayer of thanks for God's Word, such as:

   God, we thank you for revealing yourself to us through Scripture. Your Word teaches, inspires, and gives us truth and life.

2. Read—Psalm 1

3. Discuss

   - What does this text actually say?
   - What does the text mean?
   - How does it apply to my life?
   - What does it reveal about God?

4. Apply: This passage talks about delighting in God's direction and meditating on it day and night. Those who do are "like a tree planted by streams of water, which yields its fruit in season."

   - What could this text actually mean to the two of you as a couple?

   _____

   _____

   _____

5. Close in prayer—Thank God for his life-giving Word. Ask him to plant a deep desire in your hearts to seek his Word daily and weave his truth into your life and marriage.

5

Loving Your Closest Neighbor

Love your neighbor as yourself.
Matthew 22:39

If you want to connect your marriage with your faith, you can't leave out the core value of unconditional love! When asked what is the most important commandment, Jesus said we are to love God with all of our heart, soul, and mind and to love our neighbor as ourself (Matthew 22:37–39). Our love for God affects our relationships on the human level, and loving your neighbor as yourself takes on a fresh new meaning when we apply it to marriage.

Who is your closest neighbor? Isn't it that person who is nearest and dearest to you—your spouse, the one you chose to share your life at its deepest and most intimate level? If we love our marriage partner as we love ourselves, we will have his or her best interests at heart, we will want to serve rather than be served, and we will resist the urge to manipulate or pull power plays. We will have a relationship based on love, trust, and service.

If we love our partner as we love ourselves, we will strive to accept each other and love one another unconditionally. In 1 Corinthians 13, Paul gave some good advice to the people of Corinth who were having trouble loving one another unconditionally. He reminded them that love is patient and kind. When you really love someone, you don't envy them or easily get angry with them. Your love will show forgiveness and will not keep track of wrongs or dwell on the other's shortcomings.

Does the love Dave and I have match Paul's description? Not always! It's hard to love like that. It's certainly not natural, and in our experience, it's the spiritual dimension of life that empowers us to live out this kind of love with each other. Dave and I have to continually realize that love is a choice we make. Sometimes we give each other unconditional love in the hard times. At other times, our love has been very conditional, but we keep trying.

Our friend Ken shares:

> For several weeks my wife, Jennifer, had looked forward to having lunch with two friends, but when the day came, our daughter, Logan, got sick and needed to stay home from school. My day was filled to the brim, so I couldn't help with Logan, but I could see how disappointed Jennifer was to miss the chance to be with her friends. As the mother of three children, it's not easy to schedule times like this, but obviously today would not happen as she had planned unless she could find someone who could stay with Logan.
>
> Close to lunchtime I got an instant message from Jennifer, saying, "It's not going to work out. I'm canceling my lunch." My last appointment had finished early and the next one had been rescheduled for later in the afternoon, giving me a pocket of free time. If I left immediately, I could get home in time to be with Logan. So I called Jennifer and said, "I'm on my way home. You'll be able to make lunch with your friends." It took

extra effort on my part to go home, but it was one way I could love and encourage Jennifer.

Ken also shared this quick story of unconditional love:

Friday evenings have been my time to play indoor soccer with friends. It's not always easy to balance family and work, and on one Friday evening I could see that Jennifer wasn't excited about my playing soccer. I offered to stay home. "No, you go," she insisted. "It's your time to relax with your friends—and you need the exercise," she said smiling.

Ken and Jennifer both freely gave the gift of love to each other. Both really appreciated the others' thoughtfulness. Both expressed thanks to the other. When your spouse encourages you, do you let him or her know you appreciate it? Do you give feedback? Look for ways you can encourage each other. Sometimes it's an action. Sometimes it's as simple as giving your partner a compliment. And as we have seen, it especially makes a difference when a couple faces hard times.

Hunting for Hope

Bill and Beth were having difficulty living out their love for each other, and Claudia and I were talking with them about refocusing and reaffirming their love for each other. It had been an intense discussion, when suddenly Bill had one of those *aha* moments. He turned to his wife and said, "Beth, even with all our difficulties over the years, we really do have a reservoir of memories full of good times together. You know, I really do like you even if sometimes I act like I don't."

Beth smiled tenderly. "Yes, you're right. We do have a lot of good memories, and it's time we built some more!"

Bingo! That was the magic moment when we knew in our hearts they had turned the corner to a more loving marriage.

They were choosing a positive path—the path of drawing on the goodwill of the past and of accentuating and cultivating the positives for the future.

We believe one key to a successful marriage is to keep the positives above the negatives. The results? Couples who like each other and enjoy being together—couples who are best friends. In our own national survey we discovered that the greatest indicator of a successful long-term relationship was the level of the couple's friendship.[1] Just like good friends often do, happier couples enjoy pursuing many leisure activities together. They have not forgotten how to be best friends. Healthy couples find ways to stay connected or get reconnected in the midst of their busy lives.

So for Bill and Beth to realize the importance of loving encouragement and goodwill in their relationship was a major breakthrough. We also observed that if they had not had that reservoir from over the years, it would have been even more difficult to rebuild their relationship. Hopefully, when you reflect on your marriage history, you can identify your own reservoir of encouragement and goodwill. If the past is scarce on these qualities, don't panic and give up. You can start today to build a better relationship. It's a choice you can make!

Skip the Negative, Accentuate the Positive

The opposite of promoting goodwill is to tear down your spouse. This is one of the most cruel and unloving things you can do—it attacks the very core of the marriage relationship. Yet we may be tearing down the other without realizing what we are doing. Here's a challenge for you. For the next twenty-four hours, track the number of positive and negative statements you make to your partner. Take note of even the sarcastic remarks that are meant to be funny. Because sarcasm combines negative comments with humor, often couples are unaware of how destructive these subtle comments can be, especially in front of others.

I (Heather) am so blessed to have a husband who is in the habit of paying me compliments, especially in front of the children. Our kids believe I am the prettiest mom and the best cook in all of Colorado! It is such a gift to know how valuable my contributions to our family are each day.

One researcher even recommends a specific level of positive comments. Dr. John Gottman, in his book *Why Marriages Succeed or Fail*, says: "You must have at least five times as many positive as negative moments together if your marriage is to be stable."

Too often in marriage, the ratio of positive to negative is one to five—not five to one. What do you think your ratio will be? Remember five to one is just staying even—a "stable" marriage.[2] Other specialists suggest that seven to one is a healthier ratio.

When we think negatively, it's easy to express our negative thoughts, and when we do have positive, tender thoughts, often we keep them to ourselves. Bring them out in the open by expressing them orally or writing them down in a love note you can pass on to your spouse.

How Do I Love You? Let Me Count the Ways

When Elizabeth Barrett Browning penned the words "How do I love you? Let me count the ways," she was giving her readers an important biblical principle—to dwell on the positive. In Date 2 we mentioned how the apostle Paul encouraged his Christian brothers and sisters to think about whatever is true, noble, right, pure, lovely, and admirable (Philippians 4:8) instead of the negative.

However, in real life, don't we often do just the opposite? Whatever is untrue, whatever is wrong or negative, those are the things we tend to dwell on.

Positive thoughts are worth developing. But be prepared to persevere; stable habits take time and persistence. Begin by thinking about your spouse and listing one thing that is true about him or her. Does your spouse demonstrate his or her love and commitment to you? How? What is one thing that is honorable? Perhaps your spouse shows integrity in business and financial affairs. Continue through Philippians 4:8, considering how your partner is noble, right, pure, lovely, and admirable.

Later, if you feel yourself moving into a negative-thinking pattern, change direction; pull out your list, and dwell on your partner's positive qualities. Negative thinking can contaminate the rest of your relationship if you don't get it under control. It is human nature to find evidence for what we believe. If we believe negative things about our partner, we will often misread their actions as intentionally harmful and assume they are motivated only by self-interest.

This negative thinking is a slippery slope. It may start with something small like the way he chews his food or the amount of time she spends on the phone with her friends. Once you see this behavior again and again, you may begin to add to the list, and before you know it, you'll have quite a laundry list of behaviors that really bother you. If you find yourself annoyed by something your spouse does or does not do, ask yourself, "How significantly does this behavior affect me?" or "Whose problem is this?" If it is something that continues to be an issue, bring it up in a loving way before it becomes a bigger issue or the start of a negative list.

Does your partner know how much you love and appreciate him or her? Now take those positive thoughts and turn them into verbal affirmation. When was the last time you complimented your spouse? If it hasn't been in the last week, get busy! In expressing love for your closest neighbor—your spouse—you may even need to go beyond verbal affirmation. In *The Five*

Love Languages, Gary Chapman identifies verbal affirmation as just one way of expressing affection. Some individuals feel even more loved through spending quality time together, receiving a gift, physical touch, or an act of service. Chapman says we often make the mistake of speaking our own "love language" to our partner instead of expressing love in the way they most appreciate. To begin understanding your partner's preference for giving and receiving love, pay attention to what he or she most often asks for and what he or she tends to give others.

Heather and I were several years into our marriage before I realized her preferred love language was last on my list! All the other ways of expressing love came easily to me, but my frugal nature made buying a gift my least favorite expression of love. The light went on one day when Heather and I were reminiscing about our dating experience prior to engagement. She was sharing some ways I had made a positive impression on her, but it was clear that a favorite memory was when I bought her a hat she wanted. We had been out on a date when she saw this particular hat in a boutique window. She commented on it and even tried it on, but didn't buy it for herself. I remembered this and went back to the store a few days later to pick it up for her. It wasn't expensive, and there was no occasion such as a birthday or anniversary attached to the gift, but that's what made it feel so special to her. I had paid attention and went out of my way to give her something she valued. Now many years into marriage, I have to remind myself that my wife really appreciates a little gift from time to time. And it doesn't have to be expensive or extravagant. The best gifts simply show her I've been thinking about her and paying attention. This doesn't come naturally to me, but it's part of loving my closest neighbor.

As for me (Heather), Peter's love language—physical touch—is quite low on my list. It even moved down a notch after having young children around who always wanted to have a little more touch time. Physical touch began to wear me out! I have to remind myself to hold Peter's hand or snuggle up to him instead of my pillows on the couch when watching a movie. I also have to remember to compliment him with words of affirmation. He does it so naturally for me, and I know it is significant, but it doesn't always come to my mind to repay the compliments.

Add Some Fun

A first cousin to encouragement is having fun together. We (the Arps) like to say that fun in marriage is serious business! One way we put more fun into our marriage is to have dates. Actually, we have developed a "dating attitude." We turn almost anything into a date. Each fall we have a flu-shot date. How could we get excited about that? Well, it's something we need to do for our health, especially since we are on the road so much leading seminars, so we simply make it a date. Being the gentleman, I hold Claudia's hand while she gets her shot and then she holds mine. We stop at our favorite coffee shop for a cup of coffee on the way home. Those things you "just have to do," you can do together and call it a date!

No one to stay with the kids? Try an at-home date night. Peter and I sometimes put the kids to bed early and then make a grown-up dinner. We even use the good dishes and light the candles. It is a great idea for a date on a budget but still feels special. Another option is to find friends with kids who would like to have a date night too. You can watch one another's kids and still stay on budget. We tell our kids when they fuss about our going on a date that the greatest gift we can give them is a strong marriage. Now that they are old enough to be aware of friends whose parents are getting divorced, they can see the value in this statement.

Dating takes a little creativity. It is more about being creative than it is about money. Remember some of the activities you enjoyed while dating or before your kids came along. Our friends who just had their third child find that sailing together is still the special treat it was when they were dating. In fact, it now gives them an opportunity to really connect with each other: no mobile phones, no kids to distract, and no one else on the boat. Sailing allows them to be quiet in each other's presence without having to dwell on the many details that keep life so busy.

We often ask our Great Dates seminar participants to share their best dates with us. Here are some suggestions:

- "We like to take the back roads, get lost, and then find our way home again."
- "Each fall we have an apple-picking date."
- "We had fun reliving our first date with each other."
- "We love to go to our favorite restaurant, order a starter and a dessert, and enjoy the jazz music."
- "We look for free concerts in the park."

One last tip: Make sure your date activity includes plenty of time to talk with each other. You can find more fun dating suggestions in the Arps' book *52 Fantastic Dates for You and Your Mate.*

Now It's Your Turn to Love Your Closest Neighbor

We have given you suggestions on how to love and encourage your closest neighbor. Now it's time to look for ways to encourage each other, to give sincere affirmation, and to push the positive. Use the following Dating Guide and enjoy celebrating your love and encouraging each other.

Loving Your Closest Neighbor

On this date you'll talk about how to love and encourage your closest neighbor—your spouse—the one you have chosen to share your life at its deepest and most intimate level.

Pre-Date Preparation

- Read chapter 5, "Loving Your Closest Neighbor."
- Preview the Date 5 Exercise (in the back of the book).
- Choose a quiet location that will allow you to talk.

Date-Night Tips

- An important part of learning to love your spouse is understanding the ways he or she feels loved and also by giving affirmation. Being intentional about discussing these things doesn't make them any less romantic.
- Your partner cannot read your mind, so don't fall victim to the myth that states "If my spouse really loves me, he (or she) will just know what I want and I won't have to ask."

Chapter Summary

You may be familiar with the great commandment that Jesus gives his disciples: "'Love the Lord your God with all your heart and with all your soul and with all your strength and with all your mind'; and, 'Love your neighbor as yourself'" (Luke 10:27). Have you ever considered your spouse to be your closest neighbor? Putting this kind of love into practice can revolutionize your marriage.

Paul describes unconditional love in his letter to the Corinthians:

> Love is patient, love is kind. It does not envy, it does not boast, it is not proud. It does not dishonor others, it is not self-seeking, it is not easily angered, it keeps no record of wrongs.
>
> 1 Corinthians 13:4–5

If you love someone, you will be loyal to him no matter what the cost. You will always believe in him, always expect the best of him, and always stand your ground in defending him. Does this sound like the kind of love you have in your marriage? We really can't love like this in our own strength. However, with God's help, we can learn!

One way to learn this kind of love is to look for the positives in your spouse and your marriage. Challenge yourself to track the number of positive comments you make to your spouse in one day. Compare them to the number of negative comments. Watch your thoughts too. If you look for negative things in your spouse, you'll be sure to find them. Instead, fix your thoughts on what is true, good, and right, and dwell on the fine things in others. This too is truth from God's Word found in Philippians 4:8.

There are many ways to show love to your spouse. In *The Five Love Languages*, Gary Chapman identifies five ways to show love: words of encouragement, quality time, acts of service, physical touch, and receiving gifts. Identify your spouse's love language and then take the time to demonstrate that love to him or her. Remember to create more positives in your marriage. Date your spouse. Have fun. Try some new activities or do something you enjoyed doing together early in your relationship. Creating new positive experiences with your spouse will fan the flame of love in your marriage.

Post-Date Spiritual Discovery

Loving Your Closet Neighbor

1. Pray—Open with a prayer, thanking God for his love, such as:

   Lord, we thank you for the many ways you demonstrate your love for us. Teach us to follow your example as we learn to love you and each other more each day.

2. Read—Ephesians 4:29; Proverbs 15:1; 1 Peter 3:9; James 1:19

3. Discuss—Our words are powerful and can be used for encouragement or destructive criticism.

   • Think about the first words you say to your spouse each day. Are they words of encouragement or words of criticism?

   • How do you respond if your partner says or does something hurtful?

   • How would you like to respond?

   • What wisdom from the passages listed above most stands out to you?

4. Apply—List some ways you can encourage your spouse this week.

   • How can your words be a blessing—good and helpful—so that your words will be an encouragement to those who hear them?

   • What kind of nonverbal encouragement could you give this week?

5. Close in prayer—Thank God for his love, patience, and grace. Pray that his Spirit will fill you this week and give you the grace to love each other as Scripture teaches. Ask him to help you speak to one another in an honoring and helpful manner this week.

6

Talking Together With God

Do not be anxious about anything, but in every situation, by prayer and petition, with thanksgiving, present your requests to God.

Philippians 4:6

While speaking to a group about growing together spiritually as a couple, Heather and I asked why praying together can be difficult. We anticipated answers such as "not enough time" or "feeling uncomfortable." Then one couple bravely told us, "It never occurred to us that we *should* pray together." We welcomed their honesty, and it's true, praying together doesn't come naturally for some couples.

As we (the Arps) mentioned earlier, when we got married, Claudia wanted to pray together more than I did. In retrospect, she admits she became somewhat of a "prayer nag." I knew we should pray together, but I was reluctant. Claudia was more verbal than I was and fluent in "spiritual talk." When I finally agreed to pray with her, Claudia started praying about this and that. All the while I was thinking, *What can I pray about?* Before I knew it, Claudia had covered my concerns as well. So when she finally finished praying, I simply said, "Amen."

She looked at me with disappointment, and asked, "Dave, aren't you going to pray too?"

"You covered it all," I responded. This was not a marriage builder! I certainly didn't want to try that again!

Eventually I agreed to try praying together again. While I got in a few words, we both from time to time used prayer as an underhanded way to tell the other person what he or she was doing wrong, such as, "Please help Claudia understand how to better meet my needs," or "Please help Dave be more thoughtful and help more around the house."

You can see where this sort of praying was headed. We were both frustrated with each other and were about to give up on praying together when a more mature friend gave us some helpful suggestions. But before we share them with you, here is the Larsons' experience of trying to pray together.

Heather's Answered Prayer

Our prayer life as a couple has been an answer to prayer! I (Heather) remember when Peter and I were first married. I just assumed we would be praying together daily. After all, he had been working with a Christian youth ministry leading kids in prayer and devotions. I was so taken aback when Peter told me, "Prayer is very personal and something I would feel more comfortable doing alone." He was really not even open to discussing it.

I didn't know what to do or how to change his mind, but I was meeting with a wonderful godly woman at the time. I complained to her about Peter's unwillingness to pray together. "How do I get him to change his mind?" I asked her. She quickly recognized that I was looking for advice on how to convince Peter that I was right and he was wrong.

Instead, she wisely told me, "Be patient. Only God can change Peter's heart. Pray for God to give Peter the desire to pray together in your marriage." It wasn't easy to resist the temptation to bring this up and complain about it, but I began praying for this change to take place in his heart, inspired by God and not me.

Several years passed, but I still remember the day Peter came home from work all excited about some new research. "Have you heard that couples who pray together have a better chance of staying married and even a better sex life?" These were just the facts that Peter needed to change his heart. He wanted to start praying together right away. It took five years for him to realize this, but it was worth the wait.

It was hard to contain my joy and not say, "I told you so!" In fact, I waited quite some time before reminding Peter of my request early on in our marriage and how our prayer time together was an answer to my prayers.

This doesn't mean it was easy for us to begin praying together. We had to experiment with various approaches and times that worked best for us. And in the years since, it has not always been easy to stay consistent with daily prayer as a couple, but we continue to feel blessed with a closer spiritual connection when we do.

Prayer Is Talking With God

"Dave and Claudia," our friend told us, "couple-prayer is simply talking with God together. You aren't trying to communicate with each other, but together, communicate with God. You need to forget the spouse improvement requests and pray about mutual concerns."

Then he gave us some simple yet helpful advice. He suggested that before Dave and I pray together, we make a list of things we want to pray about. Next, we take turns praying through the list. To be honest, it took practice, but it worked for us and perhaps will work for you too. Now, when we pray together, we don't always make a list before we pray, but still at times, list-making is the best approach.

"God, the best maker of all marriages, combine your hearts in one," wrote William Shakespeare in *Henry V*. And one way that God combines our hearts in one is through the discipline of prayer.

Our friends David and Jan Stoop, authors of *When Couples Pray Together*, are prayer champions and have encouraged us over the years to pray together as a couple. In their book they write, "We've all heard that 'the couple who prays together stays together.' It's true, praying together does more than bring two people into the presence of the living God, as powerful as that is! It also knits two hearts together."[1]

That's certainly been the experience of our friends Emma and Adrian:

> When we first married, Emma and I made a covenant with each other that we would not go to bed at night without praying together. Fourteen years later, we're still abiding by our covenant, and I can't tell you the times our commitment not to go to bed without praying together has had an impact on our relationship. Whenever we have issues or are upset with each other, we both know we can only avoid it for up to twelve hours or so. We have to deal with it before we can pray together and go to bed.

If praying together can promote spiritual closeness in marriage, why don't more couples do it? When Dave and I began trying to pray together, it wasn't always easy, even with prayer lists. It was a process, and it took time to feel comfortable praying aloud together.

If you haven't been praying together, it may not be easy to open up your prayer life to your partner. After all, this is an intimate aspect of your Christian life that previously was shared only between you and God. Plus, God loves you unconditionally and isn't critical. Adding a third prayer partner can feel uncomfortable. Will your partner criticize the way you pray? Will you reveal your weaknesses and insecurities? Isn't three a crowd? Will this really work?

Yes, say the Stoops. "We've found that praying together is one of the most powerful things we can do to develop spiritual intimacy as a couple." But the Stoops encourage couples to start small. They suggest starting with five or ten minutes at the most and to begin by praying together silently and holding hands so that when you are finished you can squeeze your partner's hand, and when they finish, they can squeeze back.[2]

Actually, this is the Quaker model of prayer, where you share silently together. This allows each of you to worship according to your own personal needs, to seek communion with God separately and privately, yet be supported by the awareness that your spouse is also sharing in the experience. It's an easy first step in praying and worshiping together. According to the Quaker tradition, the devotional time is appropriately concluded with the kiss of peace.

The 10-Minute Miracle

At a 10 Great Dates seminar, a couple came up to us during a break. "We've been married for eleven years twice!" the wife told us. "Eleven bad years followed by eleven good years. We actually got remarried." The husband explained, "Several years ago we paid a thousand dollars to a professional counselor. His suggestion to pray together daily was by far the best learning we took away from that interaction. It has changed our relationship at the deepest, most significant and lasting level. God is the miracle worker!"

The couple then shared the following 10-minute prayer pattern. Feel free to modify it to make it your own. The vital ingredient is daily prayer time together!

5 minutes—Scripture reading

2 minutes—one prays

2 minutes—the other prays

1 minute—silence before the Lord

Monday, Wednesday, Friday—husband takes the lead

Tuesday, Thursday, Saturday—wife takes the lead

Sunday—the Lord leads[3]

This "prescription" saved one marriage. Perhaps it can save yours, and it's free!

Developing a Couple Prayer Life

The Stoops give three suggestions on how a couple can enjoy a prayer life together:[4]

1. *Praying Scripture for each other.* Suggested passages included Philippians 1:9–10 and Ephesians 1:18–21. Dave and I have a favorite praise CD that we keep in our car. The praise songs are Scripture set to music. Sometimes just listening to this music in an attitude of prayer promotes spiritual intimacy.

2. *Writing out prayers and then sharing them with each other.* This is a good way to begin to pray out loud with each other. Keep your written prayer short, simple, and meaningful to you. Then come together and read your prayers

to each other. Afterward you can share your responses
with each other. How did you feel as your partner was
reading the prayer, and how did it feel to talk aloud to
God together?

3. *Praying as you talk.* After you are more comfortable praying together, the Stoops suggest that prayer can become a
natural part of your conversations together. Often when
Dave and I are walking and talking, one of us will suggest, "Let's pray about this right now." It's an affirmation
that God is present in our conversations and gives us the
freedom to spontaneously pray informally together. It can
also be less threatening to pray when you're walking and
not facing each other.

Another suggestion is to pray the words of favorite hymns
and praise songs. Prayer is more than making our requests to
God. Together, we (the Larsons) also want to thank God for
his love and provision and to give him praise and honor. Peter's
dad kept a hymnal near his favorite chair. As he looked at the
woods in the backyard, he would read the words of his favorite
hymns in praise and adoration of our Creator.

Find the time that works best for you. Some couples get up
early for daily devotions and prayer. Other couples will make
time during the day. Heather and I have found that bedtime is
a great opportunity for us to pray together. When the lights go
out, we hold hands and take turns praying, bringing our requests
and praises before the Lord.

Honest and sincere prayer is powerful. It requires vulnerability, humility, and sincerity to come before the Lord, confessing,
praising, and making our deepest desires and requests known
to God and to one another. In these moments, there can be a
profound level of intimacy.

If you're looking for a resource with prayers to help you get
started, you may want to look at *The Book of Common Prayer*

or *A Guide to Prayer for All God's People.* Other options can be found by searching the Internet for "books on prayer" and finding a resource that fits for you.

Prayer and Conflict

Prayer can also force couples to do a gut check and address the condition of their hearts. When there is tension or conflict in marriage, couples tend to build walls and close off their hearts toward one another. But prayer requires a certain level of openness for honest mutual participation. If you find yourself unwilling to pray together, this may be a sign that some repair work needs to be done on your relationship. You can't face off against each other in conflict while kneeling before the Lord side by side; it's simply too incongruent. Praying together often forces a change in posture, both internally and externally.

In his research on faith-based couples, Professor Mark Butler and his colleagues found prayer to have a powerful impact on marital conflict. In two separate studies, couples reported how the experience of prayer during times of conflict helped them soften their attitudes, provided a healing perspective, facilitated empathy, increased a self-change focus, and encouraged the couples' responsibility for problem solving. Participants in these studies also indicated how prayer fostered the experience of a relationship with God, in a way inviting him into the tough discussions. These studies suggest that marriage therapists should indeed consider the use of prayer as an intervention and skill for couples in conflict.[5]

Where Intimacy Intersects

Intimacy can be experienced in many ways, but there is a powerful relationship between spiritual, emotional, and physical intimacy, particularly for women, who are typically more tuned in to how close and connected a relationship feels. So when a spiritual and emotional connection is established, transitioning to physical intimacy feels quite natural.

Psychologist and author Gary Oliver prescribes daily prayer for couples he sees in his practice whenever they have problems with their sex life. He strongly believes that spiritual and physical intimacy are interconnected, and you can't address one type of intimacy without acknowledging the other. Who knew prayer could improve your love life?

A Day of Prayer

As you get more comfortable praying together, you can expand your prayer time. We (the Arps) still remember a special day when we were living and working in Vienna, Austria, and sensed that it was time to consider returning to the United States. Our boys were older and really wanted to go to university in the States. We had completed the development of the marriage curriculum for German-speaking countries that had been our major project during our years in Austria. So many decisions, so much to think and pray about! So we decided to dedicate one whole day to prayer. We prayed together. We prayed separately. We made many lists and prayed through our lists. At the end of the day we felt connected to each other and to God and expectantly awaited his leading and direction in our decision to move back to the United States.

Prayer Notebook

Another prayer tradition we established years ago was making a yearly prayer list for ourselves, for each other, and for each of our children. Together we talked about what we wanted to pray for in our children's lives and in ours. We each made our own prayer notebook, and as we prayed together (and individually) during the year we kept a running diary where we recorded our prayers and answers. How encouraging to go back years later and see how God worked and answered our prayers.

Informal Times of Prayer

Once we established the habit of praying together, we found that some of our best times of prayer often happened spontaneously. We walk together several times each week and have found this is a great time to pray together. Out in nature, we feel so in tune with each other and with God. Also, car time is another opportunity to pray together. We now live in the Washington, D.C., area, and with the incredible traffic, we have a lot of time in the car together.

Look at your own life and you will be able to find little pockets of time to pray together informally. Our prayer for you is that you will discover that praying with your partner will pull you together and promote more spiritual intimacy with each other and with God.

Getting Started

Sometimes praying out loud with someone can feel intimidating. You may wonder, *How should we start a prayer? How will we know when we are finished?* Although there is no formula to prayer, it may be helpful to have some guidelines. Using the acronym ACTS can give you a format that will help keep you on track.

> A: *Adoration*—Praise God for who he is and what he has done. You can use Scripture to guide you as you both acknowledge who God is.

C: *Confession*—This will feel like a natural response after taking time to praise the God of the universe. The Holy Spirit will bring to light areas where you need to confess sin.

T: *Thanksgiving*—This can be the beginning of your "list" together, thanking God for the specific blessings in your life.

S: *Supplication*—Continue with your requests before the Lord.

You can try praying together in a variety of ways. You may hold hands side by side or pray while you are walking. Try praying on your knees. This posture together before the Lord made a huge impact on our prayer life. Remember, this isn't a contest to see who can be the most eloquent, but an opportunity to take your spiritual and marital relationship to a new level of intimacy.

Peter and I (Heather) brainstormed a list of ways to pray together to help couples discover their comfort level. See where you are on the list. Start there. Then you can encourage each other to take prayer to a deeper level in your relationship.

1. Share a list of prayer requests with each other.
2. Agree to pray for one another—separately.
3. Pray silently together.
4. Read a prayer, hymn, or Bible passage.
5. Take turns praying out loud—one person per day.
6. Both have a turn praying aloud.
7. Keep a prayer journal together.
8. Pray conversationally as you walk or hike.
9. Hold hands as you pray out loud.
10. Pray together on your knees.
11. Have a day of prayer or prayer retreat.

Time for a Great Prayer Date!

We hope some of our couple-prayer suggestions will resonate with you. Let us encourage you to take the risk to step out in faith and develop the habit of talking to God together. Couple-prayer is a wonderful experience and can bring you closer to each other and to God. It can become a vital part of your faith walk together.

Now use the following Date 6 Guide and get ready to talk about how you would like to craft your own couple prayer life.

Great Date 6

Talking Together With God

On Date 6 you'll talk about how to overcome obstacles to praying together as a couple and practical ways to develop a more meaningful prayer life together.

Pre-Date Preparation

- Read chapter 6, "Talking Together With God."
- Fill out the Date 6 Exercise (in the back of the book).
- Choose a location where you can talk privately—maybe a park or a chapel.

Date-Night Tips

- In praying, take turns, and keep your sentences short and simple, allowing the other to join in.
- Praying together is very personal. Remember, you're talking with God. Don't use prayer as an opportunity to give your partner a message (e.g., "God, help my spouse to be more sensitive to my needs").

Chapter Summary

You may have heard the saying that couples who pray together, stay together. We have good news: It's true! However, it's not always easy, especially if you haven't tried praying together before. You may be in a relationship where one of you is more eager than the other to pray together. This can be a challenge. You may be tempted to become a "prayer nag" or use prayer as a way to suggest spouse improvements. Neither of these methods will do much to encourage couple-prayer. Why not try praying for prayer in your marriage? Pray for both of your hearts to be open to praying together.

Once you're ready to pray together, you may want to create a prayer list. You can take turns praying through the list together. This way you both will get a chance to participate, and those who are more apt to "take over" the prayer are kept in check. Prayer lists can also be used to look back to see how God has been faithful to answer your prayers. Maybe you want to start by simply praying silently together and holding hands. You can give the other a squeeze when you have finished, or try writing out your prayers and reading them together. Praying Scripture aloud is another option.

Finding time to pray together can be a challenge for some couples. Some prefer the morning while others find praying in bed at night works well. If you look for pockets of time to pray together, you may be surprised at the opportunities you find. You can pray as you walk or drive together. God is listening and wants to hear from you. Praying together will create intimacy in your relationship. It is nearly impossible to come together in prayer if you are not in a good place with one another relationally. Having a regular time of prayer together can provide an incentive to do the work needed in your relationship so you are ready to come together in prayer.

Post-Date Spiritual Discovery

Talking Together With God

1. Pray—Thank God for the awesome privilege of speaking directly with him through prayer, perhaps using the following:

   Lord, we are amazed at the opportunity we have to stand in your presence and seek your face. We ask that you teach us to pray together in a way that honors you and strengthens our bond as a couple. Thank you for our many blessings.

2. Read—2 Chronicles 7:14; Matthew 18:19–20; Mark 11:25; Philippians 1:3–6; 2 Thessalonians 1:11; 1 John 5:14

3. Discuss—The passages above expose several facets of prayer.

   • Why is it humbling to seek God's face?

   • Talk about the power of coming together to pray as a couple.

   • How does couple-prayer help us address the condition of our hearts?

   • Do you make requests for each other with joy?

- What is your faith prompting you to do in your life right now? How could your spouse encourage these promptings through prayer?

- What do you believe happens when we ask for things that are not part of God's will?

4. Apply—Ask your spouse how you can be praying for him or her this week. Schedule a daily time when you can take a few moments to pray together.
5. Close in prayer—Thank God for your time together and his gift of prayer in your lives.

7

Building Your Marriage
on a Strong Foundation

We are his house, built on the foundation of the apostles and the
prophets. And the cornerstone is Christ Jesus himself.

Ephesians 2:20 NLT

In the last few dates we've considered some of our core beliefs and how to build a more spiritually intimate relationship
through experiencing God together and deepening our love for
each other. Now we want to consider the biblical foundation for
marriage. Marriage was God's idea! In the beginning he created
the first marriage, and it was very good.

Three Foundational Principles

The foundation for marriage is recorded early in the first book
of the Bible: "Therefore shall a man leave his father and his
mother, and shall cleave unto his wife: and they shall be one

113

flesh" (Genesis 2:24 ASV). From this passage we can draw three principles for a healthy marriage: leaving, cleaving, and becoming one flesh. This passage also provides direction and a foundation for a shared spiritual journey.

The importance of this passage was underscored by Jesus, who reminded his disciples and others of the passage in Genesis (Matthew 19:4–5; Mark 10:7–8). So we take these three principles seriously and hope that you will too. We are convinced they form the basis for a healthy, growing, loving marriage relationship. Let's look closer.

The Commitment to Leave

Therefore shall a man leave his father and mother . . .

Genesis 2:24 describes leaving in the context of leaving your family of origin and forming your own family unit. While we naturally think of moving out of our parents' home, it's more than that—it's also an attitude of re-prioritizing our allegiance from our parents to our partner. This is obviously much more complicated when couples live in the same house with or near their parents or extended family.

At a 10 Great Dates seminar for engaged and newlywed couples, we (the Arps) talked with Sarah and Jonathan, who were soon to be married and planned to live for a year with Jonathan's parents. Jonathan had one more year of university, and living together with his parents would help them out financially. How did Sarah feel about this arrangement? While she thought Jonathan's parents were great, we could sense some apprehension. Clearly, it would be harder for Jonathan to "leave his parents" if they were living under the same roof.

Our advice? Do with less and find a small apartment near the university. We realize that in some circumstances it's necessary for several generations to live together, so leaving is much more than a physical separation. Again, it's an attitude of refocusing on each other and making other people and things a lower priority than your spouse. Jonathan and Sarah may have found this was more difficult to do if they were living with his parents.

Peter and I (Heather) can relate to leaving our families and choosing to do with less. When we were first married, we moved from Minneapolis to Los Angeles. Peter was in graduate school, while I provided our only income as a schoolteacher. Peter was so excited when he found a creative solution to our financial situation. A generous couple allowed us to live in a finished space on the second level of their barn. In exchange, Peter fed their horses and worked in the yard one day a week.

The "apartment" in the barn left something to be desired. It was basically one room, with a tiny kitchen and bathroom tucked into one end. There were mice living in the walls and ceilings, and the old brown shag carpet was not quite what I envisioned for our first home together as a married couple. We had no television, and this was in the days before email accounts and cell phones. With no convenient or inexpensive way to stay in touch, we really were cut off from our families, who lived two thousand miles away.

We turned our attention toward one another and began fixing up the "barn." We worked hard to paint, furnish, and update the space to better fit our tastes. Peter even ripped out the carpet and installed a new floor in the bathroom. In the end, it was quite comfortable and we were proud of how we worked together to make the most of the situation. When we finished the remodel on the barn apartment, we spent many evenings hiking, biking, and playing board games. Peter always worked hard to get his studies finished during the day so we could share our evenings together. We now look back and see what a blessing it was that we were forced to leave our family of origin in

Minnesota, and in this tiny "apartment" in California, learn to cleave to each other.

When Dave and I (Claudia) were first married, we spent two years in Germany with the U.S. Army. Physically we were thousands of miles away from our parents, and as much as we loved our family, we too benefited from this time apart from them. We had the opportunity to work out our own problems and develop our own style of marriage.

Sean and Paige weren't so lucky. They came to us in a last-ditch effort to save their marriage. As they told us their story, it was obvious they had violated the basic principle of leaving. Sean was still so emotionally attached to his mom and sisters that Paige was convinced he loved them more than he loved her. When Sean had choices about how to spend his time, he chose his mom and sisters instead of Paige. Holidays had to be celebrated with his family.

While the issue of Sean's relationship with his family was a big one, it didn't stop there. Sean put his job, his friends, and his interests before his relationship with Paige, and he wasn't willing to change. Sadly, their marriage didn't make it.

Think about your own marriage relationship. How are you doing at leaving other relationships or things as less important so that you can choose to make your partner a high priority? What about your job? Have you designated your children as the higher priority? What about your hobbies, friends, or projects? What about sports? How much time do you spend surfing the Internet, reading about others on social media, or responding to emails? What about television and video games? Are you over-involved in community service activities, or are you too committed to church activities?

But before you feel guilty . . . we would probably agree that our marriage relationship should be our top priority, but in the days, hours, and minutes we have, sometimes it just doesn't work out that way. Bottom line: It's an attitude. Remember the attitude you had about your spouse when you were dating? At that time, we are often thinking of creative ways to spend more time together.

I (Heather) remember Peter telling me he just happened to "be in the neighborhood," which was more than twenty minutes from his home and work, as he stopped in to say hello. Ironically, when the time is right there in front of us, it is so easy to forget the passion we once had to spend time with each other.

Life is a delicate balancing act. Some things we can control; other things we simply must juggle. Ask yourself, if you peel off the layers of activities and time commitments, what's underneath? Do you often have wistful thoughts about your spouse? Do you use wisely the time you do have?

Now think about your own relationship. How can you creatively leave other things as less important and focus on your spouse? It's a choice you must make if you want your marriage to have a strong foundation.

The Commitment to Cleave

. . . and shall cleave to his wife . . .

Cleaving is being best friends and soul mates. It's choosing to stay together in the good times and bad times. Cleaving requires self-sacrifice—thinking of the other person and looking for ways to serve each other. In a growing, healthy marriage, each partner strives to share life on the deepest, most intimate level. What are you doing to build your friendship with your spouse? Do you share common interests and hobbies?

The closeness and connection experienced by a couple is one of the factors that best differentiates happy from unhappy couples. In the study of 50,000 marriages we previously mentioned, David Olson found the happiest couples were three times more likely to report they "felt close to each other." They made togetherness a top priority and were twice as likely to state that they enjoyed spending their free time together.[1]

Marriages are never static; they are always changing—either growing or withering. When we ignore the cleave principle and forget to concentrate on building our relationship, it's easy to get bored. We cover up by becoming over-involved in work or caring for our children. Couples can slowly drift apart over time.

Our own informal research shows that the number-one reason couples don't work on their marriages is lack of time—or perceived lack of time. A close second reason is that couples are bored with their partner and fill up their time with other activities or work—which comes full circle to keep them from investing time in their marriage. How are you choosing to invest your time? The choices you make as you read through this book will help you overcome boredom and build an enriched and fulfilled relationship with your partner.

Peter and I (Heather) have had to be creative to make quality time to spend with each other. We have arranged for child care and taken some trips for just the two of us. Early on, this meant simply getting away for one night at a bed-and-breakfast, reconnecting as we hiked and explored our way along the shores of Lake Superior. Now that the kids are older, we have ventured farther to Seattle for an extended weekend. It is after these times that I am often reminded of whom I married and why. It gives us time to "fall in love" again.

Because these outings are a bit more difficult to coordinate, they can't happen as often as we'd like, yet we still need regular time to connect. As mentioned before, in the last few years we have made a weekly date night a priority. One couple we know, whose children are older, take a daily walk after dinner. The kids are home starting on their homework, and the parents have a chance to catch up on their day and connect with one another. Now that all three of our children are in school, we meet for lunch dates. This works great and usually saves us money because we don't pay for a baby-sitter or the more expensive dinner menu items.

Daily we have opportunities to apply the cleave principle to our marriage. The daily pressures of life, the hard times as well as the good times, can help glue us together. The key is to pull together instead of apart.

Think about what types of things tend to pull you together. These are the things you want to do as often as possible. Now think about the things that tend to put distance in your relationship. Those are the things you want to avoid. For us, when we get over-committed and stressed, we tend to react to each other: We find we need to guard our schedule and avoid over-commitment. When you have a choice to make, ask yourself, "Will this bring us closer together, or will it put distance in our relationship?"

On Date 6, you talked about the importance of prayer. Praying together definitely helps the "cleaving process." So let us encourage you to look for ways to practice the cleaving principle, and you will find you will grow in intimacy—you will become best friends and soul mates.

The Commitment to Becoming One

. . . and they shall be one flesh.

Not only are we to leave and cleave, the third principle to a healthy marriage is to become one flesh. We are to become lovers. Passionate lovers. It's easy to understand that we need to work at leaving and cleaving, but we believe you have to work just as hard at building a creative love life. Most people don't consider sex in marriage as something you have to work at. We've talked to many engaged and newlywed couples who are convinced that a great sexual relationship happens naturally. And maybe it does while the passion is high. However, when married life settles down—and it will—the passion may also fade. We believe passion doesn't need to fade if we take the principle of becoming one seriously.

Sex was God's idea. He created us male and female and put the potential for passion deep within us to be experienced in the context of marriage. It is with God's blessing that we can pursue becoming passionate lovers. And it's not just for the first few years—sex is a gift we are to enjoy through all the years of our marriage.

When we (the Arps) were first married, we were still in university and had little discretionary money. Our major form of recreation and fun was making love. It didn't take us long to realize that instructions for having a great love life didn't come with our marriage license. But we were determined. Actually, we were managing quite well until the children started arriving.

When our first baby was born it was like someone rolled a hand grenade under our bed! It blew away our love life and brought mass confusion! We were exhausted. We felt incompetent. We didn't have any help or wise friends to give us advice, and our sexual relationship was assigned to the back burner.

This was fine for Claudia. She was too exhausted to care. Her greatest sexual fantasy was eight hours of uninterrupted sleep! Well, that wasn't my fantasy!

It was no surprise that our love life took a dive, and it was months before it began to recover. We never got back to the freedom and spontaneity of the pre-baby days. However, we did learn how to re-energize our love life with the little bit of time we could carve out for us.

Later, when the children were in school, we were able to find some blocks of time to again make our love life a priority. During these years we began what we called our "Monday Mornings." With the children away and having a flexible schedule, we blocked out a couple of hours each Monday morning just for us. We also began to go away for twenty-four-hour getaways without our children that really helped to energize our love life.

Then came the teenage years, which in themselves are challenging—those were the "hanging on" years for our love life. We did "hang on," and when we hit the empty nest years we were able to re-energize our love relationship again. Every stage of marriage is challenging, so wherever you are in the seasons of your marriage, you need to follow the "one flesh" principle, and that includes promoting passion and romance.

We (the Larsons) definitely relate to the challenge kids can present to a couple's love life. A main strategy we've stuck with is creating routines and schedules that allow our children to avoid getting over-scheduled and to go to bed early most nights. Our kids are still young (elementary-school age), so we have quite a bit of control over their schedules. We've made a conscious effort not to over-schedule our family life by signing the kids up for too many activities. We try to stick to just one sport or activity per child, plus piano lessons, which still feels plenty busy. We are also very supportive of an early bedtime for the kids. Some of our friends laugh at how early we get them down, usually by 7:30 or 8. But our children sleep well through the night, and this allows us several hours each evening to connect with one another. These very basic choices allow us the time we need as parents to keep our marriage and love life a priority.

We realize an early bed routine is not a fit for all families, but if you are looking for a book to bring in more structure at bedtime, we recommend *Sleep: Top Tips from the Baby Whisperer* by Tracy Hogg and Melinda Blau, and *Healthy Sleep Habits, Happy Child* by Marc Weissbluth. Again, our encouragement is to find a resource that fits your personality and beliefs.

How can you rekindle the spark and add romance and excitement to your love life? How can you keep love alive throughout the seasons of your marriage? You have to work at it and follow the principle in Genesis 2:24 to "become one flesh." God created the sexual union to be experienced within the framework of a loving marriage. Sex is a gift from God to you for your enjoyment and pleasure as well as for procreation. Throughout marriage, a fulfilling sexual relationship takes effort, understanding, and time! Both partners should feel free to initiate lovemaking.

What are you doing to turn your marriage into a love affair? Your sex life can be as fulfilling and exciting as you want to make it. While it takes time and work to be a creative lover, it's worth it. Your love life can become better, more intimate, and more wonderful as the years go by, and it's all with God's blessing.

Oneness in marriage also gives the picture of two persons joining together to form a sacred partnership—growing together in your love relationship and enjoying one another completely. Any pain, hurt, insult, any lack of support or faithfulness, any failure to help your partner will reflect back on your marriage partnership. Any joy, compliments, faithful support, successes, or blessings also reflect back on your marriage partnership.

We (the Arps) had just completed our session on becoming one when Vera came up to us and excitedly said,

> I only thought about becoming one physically, but now I see we can have a real sense of oneness in other areas of our marriage. This concept opens up a new understanding of intimacy in marriage. Also, it challenges me to promote the good things in our marriage and avoid the negatives. I see now how everything affects our relationship because we are partners.

Vera is right. We can be the most positive influence in our spouse's life and our spouse in ours if we are willing to choose to base our marriage on these three principles of leaving, cleaving, and becoming one.

The Three Sides of Love

Marital researchers affirm the importance of the foundational principles found in Genesis 2:24. Robert J. Sternberg, professor of psychology and education at Yale University, has an interesting theory of love and how we express it. He doesn't cite biblical truths, yet he sees love as a triangle whose three sides are commitment (leaving), intimacy (cleaving), and passion (becoming one). Let's take a closer look.[2]

Commitment (Leaving)

Commitment is the cognitive side of love. It started at nothing when you first met, but grew as you got to know each other. Sternberg says commitment is a short-term decision to love another person and a long-term decision to maintain that love. Commitment is one element of love that is desperately missing in many marriages today. Removing the option of divorce is one way to keep focus.

Intimacy (Cleaving)

Intimacy is the emotional aspect of the love triangle. It includes the closeness and sharing in marriage: intimate conversations; sharing our time, energy, and deepest feelings with each other; and giving our unconditional support to each other. Intimacy develops slowly over the years, without fanfare; each becomes the other's trusted best friend and confidant.

Passion (Becoming One)

Passion is the motivational side of love. It is the intense desire to be united physically with the person you love. Unlike intimacy, passion is a rapidly growing, hot, heavy experience. You don't even have to know the other person to feel passionate. In a real-life marriage, passion may be up and down and level off. That doesn't mean it's not there, but you may need to cultivate it.

Becoming one

Balancing Your Triangle

If you want your marriage to remain strong, we believe your foundation must include leaving (commitment), cleaving (intimacy), and becoming one (passion).

Do you see these three principles functioning in your marriage? How balanced is your own triangle? Does one side need more work than the others? How can you find a comfortable balance?

In the marriage relationship, what really matters to us in the short run—physical attractiveness, chemistry, and romance—may not matter most in the long run. Things you thought were kind of cute may begin to grate on you over the long haul. Spouses continually need to be willing to change and adapt to each other, to forgive each other, and to let their love grow into a mature, lasting love relationship.

In his research, Sternberg discovered that among the things that increase in importance over the years is simply the willingness to change in response to each other and to tolerate one another's quirks. Flexibility and a willingness to adapt are key components of a successful marriage. The most satisfied couples are significantly more likely to compromise when problems arise, adjust well to change, and find creative ways to handle their differences.[3] In our (the Arps') marriage history of more than forty years, we have learned that we can't change each other, we can only change ourselves. Interestingly, when one of us changes, the other tends to change too.

Research reveals that over the years, sharing of values—especially religious values—becomes increasingly important. The things that tend to diminish over the years (this is not very encouraging) are the ability to communicate, physical attractiveness, having good times together, sharing interests, the ability to listen, respect for each other, and romantic love. But this doesn't have to happen to your relationship—not if you have built a strong foundation.

Affirming Your Foundation

If leaving, cleaving, and becoming one are foundational principles in your marriage, you will have a growing, vibrant relationship. But you must be willing to share the load, to build a partnership. It doesn't happen automatically. Marriage is a process. Like a soccer game, there are no time-outs. A priority marriage is not a one-time decision but a daily choice. We daily choose to leave, cleave, and be one. We still are complete individuals; we still care about others, our careers, our family and friends; but daily we choose to make our marriage the key relationship in our lives. Then when difficulties come along (and they will at times), if you have a firm foundation, your marriage will more than survive. Your marriage will thrive.

Now, it's time for Date 7. Use the following Dating Guide to help you affirm the foundation of your marriage. Remember, God created marriage, and it can be very, very good!

Great Date 7

Building on a Strong Foundation

On this date you will talk about three fundamental principles for building a strong foundation for your marriage—leaving, cleaving, and becoming one.

Pre-Date Preparation

- Read chapter 7, "Building Your Marriage on a Strong Foundation."
- Review the Date 7 Exercise (in the back of the book).
- Choose a location that will allow you to talk.

Date-Night Tips

- Discuss the exercise, one point at a time.
- Concentrate on what strengthens the foundation of your marriage.
- Celebrate what you are doing right (like experiencing these dates)!

Chapter Summary

In the last few dates, we've considered some core beliefs and how to build a more spiritually intimate relationship through experiencing God together and deepening our love for each other. Now we want to consider the biblical foundation for marriage. Marriage was God's idea! In the beginning, he created the first marriage, and it was very good. He gave three fundamental principles that help us have a strong foundation for marriage. That foundation for marriage is recorded in the beginning of the first book of the Bible: "Therefore shall a man leave his father and his mother, and shall cleave unto his wife: and they shall be one flesh" (Genesis 2:24 ASV). From this passage, we can draw three principles to keep a marriage growing and healthy—leaving, cleaving, and becoming one flesh. This passage also provides direction and a foundation for our shared spiritual journey.

The principle of "leaving" is the cognitive decision to commit to your marriage. It is choosing to make your spouse a priority over family, friends, jobs, screen time, sports, or hobbies. Even good things like church activities can take time away from investing time with your spouse. "Cleaving" is the idea of being best friends with your spouse. This requires an attitude of self-sacrifice. Marriages are not stagnant. Many people divorce because they are bored in their marriage and no longer spend the time needed to create emotional closeness with one another. The third principle, "becoming one flesh," is God's plan for married couples to be passionate lovers for a lifetime. When first married, passion may be strong, but throughout different stages of marriage, you may find that this passion takes effort, understanding, and time.

To build on this biblical foundation, remember, the only person you can change is yourself. You need to be flexible and willing to adapt to your spouse. Choose daily to leave, cleave, and be one.

Post-Date Spiritual Discovery

Building on a Strong Foundation

1. Pray—Open with a prayer, thanking God for his gift of marriage:

   Lord, you are the author and creator of marriage. Help us to live in a way that honors you and your design for our marriage. Thank you for this gift.

2. Read—Matthew 19:3–11

3. Discuss—In this passage, Jesus is very clear and direct about marriage and divorce.

   • What does this passage reveal about Jesus' stance toward the bond between a husband and wife?

   • How does our current culture seem to reflect the same question asked by the Pharisees in verse 3?

   • Jesus points out that Moses only permitted divorce because their hearts were hard. What makes a heart hard?

   • What is the condition of your heart toward your partner?

   • The disciples conclude in verse 10 that it is better not to marry. Do you agree? Does Jesus agree?

- In verse 11, Jesus contends that accepting this teaching hinges on receiving help from God. Have you ever asked God for his help in fostering a strong marriage bond?

4. Apply—Ask God to help you this week as you live out your marriage commitment. In which of the three areas discussed (leaving, cleaving, becoming one) do you need the most help?

----

5. Close in prayer—Ask God for his help accepting his teachings on marriage and becoming the kind of spouse who is committed and consciously aware of the biblical foundations for marriage.

8

Facing the Storms of Life Together

I have told you these things, so that in me you may have peace. In this world you will have trouble. But take heart! I have overcome the world.

John 16:33

The gentle breeze, laden with the scent of rose geraniums, came through the open window as we (the Arps) lunched with our friends. Jack looked tenderly at Claire as he helped pull her sweater over her shoulders and she smiled back at him. Such love. Such intimacy. For us, this was amazing.

For the past fifteen years Claire had been in and out of hospitals, interspersed with days, months, and years of no energy, poor health, and little hope of ever being completely well again. The doctor's puzzlement as to the diagnosis of her condition is still a constant frustration.

But on this lovely spring day we were celebrating Claire's improving health. When we asked them how they had coped the past fifteen years, Jack answered, "We take life one day at a time."

Claire continued, "God has been so good to us. We've learned so much about his faithfulness. My illness has actually brought us closer together."

No complaints. No bitterness. Fifteen years of struggles, yet no evidence of anger or resentment.

Dave and I looked at each other and wondered if we could face such adversity with as much strength as Jack and Claire demonstrated. It's usually after the storm that we are brave and see God's hand in the hard times we have experienced. If we could just remember in the middle of the storm that God is ever present and in control, then the storms of life might bring us closer together spiritually.

Seeing God Through the Fog

On another occasion, Dave and I had looked forward to a lovely drive through the Rocky Mountains, only to have it ruined by a heavy blanket of fog. Then an amazing thing happened. The dreary sky hiding the mountain peaks gradually became brighter—and in one magical moment the fog at the very top of the mountains lifted and Dave and I could see the splendor of the snowcapped Rockies. The next moment they disappeared—as if they were playing hide-and-seek with us. Fog. Splendor. Fog. Splendor.

How breathtaking it was when the fog lifted and we could see the majestic Rockies! Then how disappointing when the thick fog reappeared! Isn't this how life is sometimes? Even on occasions in our marriage? At times, we see so clearly the beauty all around us—and at other times, we only see the fog. Yet like the Rockies in the fog, the beauty is always there whether we can see it or not!

As we continued to drive through the Rockies, we talked about times we have felt close to God and other times when we felt only distance. And then God seemed to speak to our hearts: *I am there even when you don't see me! Trust me in the foggy times as well as the sunny times in your life and in your marriage.*

Oh, if we could only remember this lesson—especially when we're in a fog of discouragement. God is there in the fog just as he is there when all is sunny in our lives. We need to trust him both times. We promised each other we would remember this day, and in those times when the fog reappears, we will remind each other that in the midst of the darkness and dullness, God is still there—even when we don't feel his presence! His love and protection—more majestic than the Rocky Mountains—surrounds us! Then we will also remember one of our favorite verses: "As the mountains surround Jerusalem, so the LORD surrounds his people both now and forevermore" (Psalm 125:2).

When the Answer Is "No, Not Now"

Peter and I learned this valuable lesson of God's faithfulness as we began the journey of becoming parents. We had been married a few years and decided it was time to start a family. Both of us are used to working hard, accomplishing goals, and getting the results we want and expect. We assumed that becoming parents would follow this pattern. We had so much to learn.

We were so excited when we found out that I was pregnant. I began reading every book on expecting a baby. We knew at our first doctor's visit that we should be able to see a little peanut-sized baby and be able to hear its heartbeat. When the ultrasound technician moved the wand, she found the sac for the baby, but no baby. We learned later that this is called a "blighted ovum." To us, it just meant much heartbreak, fear, and sadness.

During this time, we went through many stages of grief, and not always at the same time. The fact that we weren't always experiencing the same response to the storm allowed us to encourage each other and grow deeper with one another. I remember my initial personal stage of anger. I was so angry at God for allowing such a thing to happen to me. How could he not give me my heart's desire? I remember thinking, *God doesn't know what it's like to be a mother and lose a child.* Then, of course, I thought of Jesus. God knows so much more about the death of a child! I realized that God could use this circumstance to show himself to me more deeply. Peter was still hopeful, and he took comfort in the fact that many couples experience miscarriages with their first pregnancy.

Unfortunately, the journey to parenthood didn't end there. It was two more years and two more miscarriages. I remember how during this time God used his Word to comfort me. I found Psalm 71 to be a great source of hope. Verse 20, in particular, reminded me that God would not leave me in despair: "Though you have made me see troubles, many and bitter, you will restore my life again."

When we were given the news that we would be having a third miscarriage, I remember turning to this Psalm to find comfort. I remember Peter going through his stage of anger as he muttered, "Are we going to praise God through this one too?"

During this time, God drew us to him, but also to one another. We grieved and loved together in ways we didn't know were possible. We prayed and poured out our hearts to the Lord. Looking back, this was not something I would want to experience again, but I am a different person, mother, and wife because of it. I am glad I know the strong hands of God hold me and love me, even when the answer is "No, not now."

Preparing for Storms and Lessons

We all experience disappointments, hurts, and misunderstandings. Storms in life are no respecter of persons. The key is to prepare for them before they come.

After all, Jesus tells us, "In this world you will have trouble. But take heart! I have overcome the world" (John 16:33). He doesn't say *if* we have trouble, but that we *will* have trouble. The apostle Paul reminds us to be prepared for these trials by putting on the full armor of God. In his letter to the Ephesians, he encourages them to "take up the helmet of salvation and the sword of the Spirit, which is the word of God. And pray in the Spirit on all occasions with all kinds of prayers and requests" (Ephesians 6:17–18). Yes, using Scripture and prayer is the best way to prepare for the storms of life.

Perhaps you've heard the saying "All sunshine and no rain makes a desert." Naturally, we prefer the sunny times in life to the rain and storms, but God uses both times to help Peter and me grow and connect spiritually as a couple.

As we face the storms in our lives, we find the deepest and sweetest communion with the Lord and with each other. Think back to the last time you experienced a storm in your life. Can you see the ways God used that storm to teach you a new truth or to bless you? Or maybe you are in the middle of a storm right now, and it's too soon to see God's blessings. We want to encourage you to take comfort and to have hope in God's faithfulness.

Keeping Our Eyes on God

As you face the storms in your life, it is important to remember that God is good all the time. We live in a fallen world, where there is cancer, greed, corruption, and accidents. The truth is that God can redeem difficult situations and bring growth and new possibilities out of bad circumstances. After our three failed pregnancies, Heather and I were beginning to wonder if we would ever become parents. Instead, God led us to a doctor we met through our church. He put Heather on a small dose of a common medication, stating, "Sometimes this works in cases like yours, and we don't even know why."

Three years later, we had three children! I remember reading an article about prayer just as our third child, Anna, was on the way. The main point was sometimes we pray for an apple, and God gives us an orchard instead! I was overwhelmed by how profoundly true that sentiment had become in our own lives. Together, we praised God for his faithful answer to our prayers and the blessing of three healthy children. We even joked about having three children under the age of three and said, "How do we make it stop now?"

I (Heather) remember the joy of God blessing us with a family, but more storms loomed just around the corner. We were living in Branson, Missouri, and I was eight months' pregnant with our third child. We had recently sold our property in Minnesota to buy our dream home in Branson, resolved that we were going to live there and raise our family.

Suddenly things began to unravel at Peter's work. It quickly became clear that the organization he was working for was not going to be able to sustain its current structure. We were not sure if Peter was going to have a job, if we would have health insurance, or how we were going to make it with three small kids and a new house payment.

Interestingly, Peter began to get calls from two companies in Minnesota who wanted to meet with him about job opportunities. I remember the specific morning in my quiet time as I prayed about our situation, and how God gave me a picture of what was to come. God assured me we were about to be pushed off a cliff, but that he would catch us. I am not one for heights. I don't bungee jump. I don't even like balconies on tall buildings. I knew we were going to experience this fall, but I knew God would catch us. I remember God teaching me to trust him even when I couldn't see the outcome.

God did catch us from that fall, and the blessings have been more than we could ever have planned or hoped for ourselves. He took what looked like a storm that could wipe us out and turned it into an amazing opportunity. The fall turned out to be the push we needed to continue to move forward into God's plan for our life and ministry. Keeping our eyes on God and his goodness can help us keep perspective in a storm.

Learning Lessons From Past Storms

Recently we (the Arps) took the same hike in the Austrian Alps that we took several years ago right before our move to Virginia. As Claudia and I hiked, we talked about how crisis times pull us closer to each other and to God.

We immediately thought of the crisis we were facing several years ago as we were hiking this same path. We were in the middle of moving to northern Virginia from Tennessee and had come to Europe for several weeks—a mixture of work and pleasure. Having thought we had all the myriad details of our move sorted out and resolved before we left, we flew to Europe to lead conferences and to grab a few days' hiking in the Austrian Alps. But soon after we arrived in Europe, circumstances back home changed and our previous arrangements no longer worked for everyone. Without boring you with the details, we found ourselves in the middle of a misunderstanding and a huge crisis.

There we were in Austria, and all we could do was to try to sort it out with long-distance phone calls, emails, and many prayers. It was the latter that made the real difference. As we hiked, we poured out our hearts to the Lord and asked for wisdom and direction. The more we prayed, the higher we hiked, until we came to the snow line and could go no farther.

On this more recent hike, there was no snow and we weren't facing the trauma of a move, but other concerns were on our hearts. Still, remembering the stress of several years ago actually brought us closer spiritually.

As we climbed higher, we thanked God for answers to our crisis those years ago. We prayed again for everyone who had been involved in our move, and thanked God for the good that had resulted in our moving to Virginia. Our hearts were full of thankfulness, and we were stronger because of the storms we'd weathered together in the past. Also, as we prayed about our current concerns, we had a quiet assurance that the same God who answered our prayers concerning our move several years ago was with us and heard and answered our prayers today.

Turn the pages to the Date 8 Dating Guide and celebrate how God has protected you through the storms of your life and thank him for his love and care in the storms yet to come.

Great Date 8

Facing the Storms of Life Together

On this date you will talk about how God has protected you through the storms of your life and affirm his love and care for you in storms yet to come.

Pre-Date Preparation

- Read chapter 8, "Facing the Storms of Life Together."
- Preview the Date 8 Exercise (in the back of the book).
- Choose a location where you can be open to and vulnerable with each other. A quiet park or someplace you can go to be alone will provide a safe setting to discuss your past or current storms.

Date-Night Tips

- Talking about hard times in the past and the way God met your needs gives you strength and hope for the future.
- Look for ways you can support each other in "stormy weather."

Chapter Summary

Life is full of challenges and heartache that can distract us from one another and from God. Just like mountains hidden in fog, God is there for us, even when it is difficult to see him. Sometimes our prayers are answered with a no or "not now." It is during these disappointments that our faith is given an opportunity to grow. Our responses to difficult circumstances may not be the same as our spouse's. It is important to remember that feelings are not wrong or right, and not to judge but encourage each other.

Putting on the armor of God is the best way to prepare for the storms that are sure to come our way. God promises never to leave us or forsake us. Keeping our eyes on God in the storms enables us not to get lost in our circumstances, but to see God's love for us.

When we look at past storms, we can see God's faithfulness and provision. We can see his answers to prayer in unexpected ways. Past storms can give us comfort in our current situation, remembering that God's goodness and love is always behind it all.

Post-Date Spiritual Discovery

Facing the Storms of Life Together

1. Pray—Open with a prayer, thanking God for his faithfulness even in the storms of life, using words like:

   Lord, thank you for walking with us through the storms of life. Thank you that you are bigger than the issues we face. May your love, grace, and truth sustain us and give us hope for the future.

2. Read—Luke 6:46–49

3. Discuss—In this passage, Jesus talks about building a solid foundation.

   • Notice in Luke 6:48 how Jesus says *when* not *if* the floodwaters rise and break against the house. What does this tell us about storms?

   • Luke 4:47 outlines three components of laying a firm foundation. What are they?

   • How are you building these three steps into your marriage?

   • What is the recipe for a weak foundation described in Luke 6:49?

4. Apply—Consider the three components of laying a solid foundation:

   • Coming to God: How are you seeking the Lord in your daily life and marriage?

   • Listen to God's teaching: What is God teaching you?

   • Following God's teaching: Are you putting his teachings into action?

5. Close in prayer—Ask God to help you build a solid foundation as an individual, couple, and family. Pray that you'll be ready for the storms of life as you stand on the firm foundation of God's leading.

9

Guarding Your Hearts
Under God's Canopy

Above all else, guard your heart, for everything you do flows
from it.

Proverbs 4:23

Having put in a hard week of work, we (the Arps) were looking
forward to a relaxing evening at a romantic restaurant. Dave
called ahead to make reservations, so when we arrived at the
restaurant and gave our name, we were surprised they didn't
have a table for us. We were both getting a little upset when the
waiter said, "Oh, you're the Hearts!" Instead of Arps, they had
reserved the table for the "Hearts"! Now, how romantic is that?

Hearts and romance do go together. In marriage, your hearts
need to be attuned to each other, and if you want to connect
your faith in your marriage, you also need to guard your heart
from the many temptations that can lead it astray.

It's doubtful that anyone wakes up and decides, *Today is the day I'm going to walk away from my marriage, destroy my family, and find someone new*. In many cases, allowing our hearts to be polluted, followed by actions that drift into questionable territory, is a slow and subtle process.

A heart that is left open to temptation, to feelings of entitlement and resentment, can become polluted. Protecting our hearts is a daily necessity. No one is immune to temptation. If we don't run from temptation, our hearts can become closed and shut off. Our heart is central to a vibrant marriage, and with God's help we can protect our heart under his canopy.

Guard Your Heart!

The Bible often refers to the heart. There are over 950 Bible verses that contain the word *heart*! God gives us the command to love him with all of our heart, soul, and strength. He goes on to say that the commands he has given are to be upon our hearts (Deuteronomy 6:5–6). These commandments are clearly stated as the basis for good living, but they are also the foundation for a great marriage.

We can see further how vital our heart is to God when he commands us to fix his words in our hearts and minds (Deuteronomy 11:18). He tells us that he searches every heart (1 Chronicles 28:9). God has the power to harden our hearts (Exodus 4:21) and to give us a new heart (Ezekiel 36:26). The Psalms promise us that we can pray for God to search our heart (139:23), create in us a pure heart (51:10), and give us an undivided heart (86:11).

Why do you suppose God is so concerned with our hearts? When our heart is outside of God's will, temptation is sure to follow. Proverbs 4:23 applies not only to our relationship with God but also our relationship with our partner: "Above all else, guard your heart, for everything you do flows from it." If we don't guard our heart, we can find ourselves where we don't want to be—like one couple who years ago made a tremendous impact on our lives as new Christians.

Failure to Guard

When Dave and I began our pursuit for spiritual intimacy with each other and with God, several Christian couples were influential in our lives, especially Laura and Jim (not their real names). Laura taught the Bible study I attended, and Jim was the leader of the couples Bible study we both attended. Their love for the Lord was obvious, and through them many others came to faith in Christ. They had a real servant attitude and were so loving and giving to us and others. We hoped that someday we could be as spiritually mature and able to help others in the way they did. They actually influenced our decision to join a Christian ministry, which led to what we are doing to this very day. If we made a list of those who have had an impact on our life, Laura and Jim's names would be near the top.

You can imagine how devastated and disappointed we were when years later we heard they had divorced. How could that happen? What happened to their spiritual intimacy? We don't know the details, and we don't know why they divorced, but we assume that one or both of them did not guard their hearts. This was a wake-up call for us to make sure we guard our hearts and that we keep seeking to connect spiritually.

Common Temptations

What is it that is tempting us and taking our focus away from serving God and one another? How can these temptations affect our marriage?

Keeping up appearances. In today's culture, it is easy to be tempted to keep up with the Joneses. Materialism can quickly creep into our hearts. With advertisements today, it is easy to think we need something more in order to be happy. I (Heather) have observed that for some women, buying clothes or redecorating their home is a hobby, done just to keep themselves occupied. For others, it is a source of esteem or a short-term coping strategy for stress. I have found that if I don't go to the mall, I don't feel the need to buy something new.

It sounds simple, but what about those catalogs that arrive in the mail each day or all the online sales announcements? Those visual images can be tempting. We can convince ourselves that we are just looking, but soon it turns to material lust. I usually put catalogs right into the recycling bin, but the other day, I decided to page through one from a furniture store. Several items were so beautiful. I had to remind myself, *I don't need any of these things to make my home or my life complete.* We can say there is no harm in looking, but it's not long before the looks turn to desire, and then we convince ourselves that we "need" that new item. The old just won't do anymore. It's a slippery slope! Of course, materialism and the desire for "things" is not necessarily gender specific. We know men who are also shopaholics. For many men, possessions can communicate status or power and be a misguided source of esteem. Materialism can quickly lead to financial struggles and stress, often cited as the top reason couples seek divorce.[1]

"Will you be my friend?" Another easy temptation involves connecting with old relationships through social networking websites. What may start as a simple chat with an old flame can easily turn into something more, especially if you are feeling disconnected or lonely in your marriage. Peter and I have both reconnected with old friends online; however, we are careful to tell each other about whom we are talking with and share

with each other about the content of our conversations. Things that are kept hidden from one another make for fertile grounds for temptation. We are careful to guard our hearts from inappropriate friendships that would threaten the high priority we place on our marriage.

The lure of visual images! As a man in today's world, it amazes me (Peter) how difficult it can be to guard our hearts from the visual images that come crashing in from the many forms of media we encounter each day. Television shows, commercials, ads in the newspaper, email, and websites—there is almost no escape from the seductive images flashing before our eyes each day. Is it any wonder recent estimates put Internet porn use by men at almost 50 percent, a statistic that holds true even for churchgoing men? Internet Filter Review (2004 and 2006) reports that the average Internet user receives 4.5 pornographic emails per day.[2] Furthermore, daily Internet searches for pornographic terms have grown to nearly 70 million.

Unfortunately, the lure of pornography is reaching many women today as well. Research indicates that over 30 percent of online pornography users are women.[3] It's a slippery slope from romance novels to videos. For women, the social stigma can make it even more difficult to reach for help. However, there are many newer resources for women who are struggling with pornography, including www.dirtygirlsministries.com and www.thepinkcross.org.

Pornography can pollute our minds and marriages with unrealistic images and expectations that leave partners feeling betrayed and belittled. It is crucial to guard our hearts from such temptation if we wish to grow together spiritually.

Obsession for power and success. Another common temptation we must guard our hearts from involves the relentless search for success. While there is nothing wrong with hard work and achievement in itself, too many marriages have been sacrificed on the altar of success. Some individuals become so obsessed with power, position, and recognition, they virtually abandon their spouse and children to pursue their careers. No raise or promotion is worth losing your marriage. In these cases, individuals must stop and ask themselves what is driving their need for achievement. Many times, they'll find an emotional or spiritual need at the root of their obsession. Until this need is truly addressed on an emotional and spiritual level, they'll remain empty and out of balance in their striving. Sometimes, guarding our heart involves slowing down and attending to the deeper wounds and needs of our hearts.

Faith and Marriage

Our world today is not very marriage friendly. Terms like *starter marriages* and billboards that say LIFE IS SHORT. GET A DIVORCE (yes, a Chicago law firm really did use them a few years ago) don't promote marriage as a spiritual commitment "until death do us part." No wonder so many couples are confused. A Gallup poll indicated that 70 percent of Americans see nothing morally wrong with divorce.[4]

However, we believe that good marriages and spirituality should go hand in hand. But in our survey on long-term marriages, we observed an alarming trend. Of those who reported that the best aspect of their marriage was the spiritual aspect, a high percentage of their other responses indicated that they were dissatisfied with their marriage relationship. It even appeared for some that their commitment to God was the main reason they were staying in their unhappy marriage. We've seen this trend in our research, using data from the Couple Checkup Inventory. In looking at hundreds of churchgoing couples, we find that spiritual beliefs are a strength nearly 85 percent of the time, but communication and conflict resolution skills are strong in only one-fourth of those couples.

What is wrong with this picture? Shouldn't our spiritual commitment improve the quality of our marriage? Shouldn't faith in God make a huge difference in our relationship with our spouse? Shouldn't our faith enhance our love for each other? Yes, absolutely!

A couple of years ago we (the Arps) spoke at an innovative church service in a suburb of Frankfurt, Germany. More than five hundred people attended the service, which was held in the largest movie theater in the area. After our presentation, one of the first questions from the audience dealt with a local bishop who was getting a divorce after twenty-five years of marriage: "How can you say God has any relevance to my life or my marriage when the bishop is divorcing her spouse who is also a pastor?"

Good question. The singer Bono, when asked about his younger years, expressed similar disappointment in the people around him: "I never had a problem with Christ. It's Christians I had a problem with."[5] Sadly, too many Christians don't live out Christlike attributes such as patience, kindness, self-control, and love, and because of this, marriages suffer. From the outside, it's easy to conclude that spirituality has no relevance to marriage and that husbands and wives should only stay together "until the death of love do us part."

God's Sacred Canopy: Our Protection From Temptation

What has happened to the high esteem marriages once enjoyed? In his book *Spheres of Love*, Stephen Post suggests that today's marriages lack what he defines as "a sacred canopy"—an affirmation of the significant foundational beliefs concerning the holy state of marriage.

Marriage was part of God's original natural order. It transcends cultures. Marriage is a serious commitment—intended to be a permanent tie—and is the foundation of the family unit. Dr. Post writes, "Marriage is an essentially mysterious union like the mystical one between Christ and the church, should be entered into reverently with the exchange of vows, and is a place where God dwells."[6]

Stephen Post's concept of a sacred canopy struck home with us. We think a sacred canopy is an essential component to a loving Christian marriage and one where couples experience spiritual intimacy.

What do you think of when you think of the word *canopy*? Our quick word study revealed these concepts: a protective covering or shelter from life's storms, a haven, a refuge, a retreat, a sanctuary, a place of safety. Would we not all desire these words to describe our marriage?

It's God's sacred canopy that elevates marriage and makes it a holy institution. Dr. Post reiterates that it is Christianity that provides marriage with the theological roots that make marriage a lifetime commitment in a world that seems incapable of anything more than "limited engagements." "Marriage fails," he writes, "for many reasons, one of which is the lack of a foundation in meanings of any ultimate significance."[7]

A Wedding Canopy

A great word picture of God's canopy over marriage was lived out at a wedding we (the Arps) attended a few years ago. Weddings are times of celebration, of joy, and of new beginnings. Each wedding is special, but this particular one, for us, was unique. Rachel and Cannon were married under a canopy. The canopy, taken from the Jewish wedding tradition, signified God's protective covering for the bridal pair. Flowers and ribbons graciously adorned the tulle canopy under which the couple would soon stand to take their vows.

Rachel, so strikingly beautiful in her elegant yet simple white wedding dress, floated down the aisle on her father's arm who, in just a few moments, would perform the dual role of Dad and clergy. He would lead the ceremony for Rachel and Cannon.

We had known Rachel for many years and had watched her grow up and transition through the adolescent years. Now a beautiful young woman, she was about to commit herself to love, cherish, and partner with Cannon for the rest of her life.

We thought of the changes they faced ahead. In a few weeks Cannon would begin medical school. Their life would be hectic and full—so very, very full. We silently prayed that God's canopy of love would protect them; that God would guide them, and that they would remain faithful to their vows taken on this day.

Then we felt a gentle nudge in our spirits: *Pray too for your own marriage and the other marriages represented here today. Pray that those who have been given this trust of marriage might prove faithful. Pray that you will keep living out your marriage under God's holy sacred canopy day by day.*

For Rachel and Cannon, their strong faith in God, expressed in their wedding vows taken under the canopy of God's love and protection, should make a difference in the coming years of their marriage.

Does your marriage have a sacred canopy? What are your beliefs and convictions that elevate your marriage? Is your marriage a lifetime commitment? Are you committed to fidelity? Whom do you ask to help hold you accountable? Are you striving to grow together spiritually? What are the distinctive marks that set your marriage apart? Is it the loving way you relate to each other? Are you committed to guarding your heart?

Creativity, Heart, and Service

Do the words *creativity*, *heart*, and *service* describe aspects of your marriage? When we think of our mentors, David and Vera

151

Mace, those words certainly fit their marriage. When others their age were retiring and rocking on their porches, they continued—well into their eighties—to speak and train couples in marriage enrichment. As a widow at ninety-two, Vera coauthored a paper with us for the United Nation's International Year of the Family. She was an amazing woman, and we will always be grateful for what she and David meant to us.

In their classic book *What's Happening to Clergy Marriages?* the Maces shared their core beliefs about marriage. These five beliefs, if adopted (and acted upon), could help you guard your hearts and affirm God's sacred canopy over your marriage.[8]

1. *We believe that it was God who brought us together in the first place.*
2. *We believe that our continuing life together is part of the divine purpose.*
3. *We believe that we have a witness to bear together.*
4. *We believe that our shared life must have a sacrificial quality.*
5. *We believe that our Christian marriage must find spiritual expression.*[8]

We challenge you to build a sacred canopy over your marriage and to guard your hearts. Then you can experience the true joy of growing together spiritually.

Now it's time for Date 9. Follow the Dating Guide and put your hearts together for a great date.

Great Date 9

Guarding Your Hearts Under God's Canopy

On this date you'll look at how to guard your heart and what it means to have God's sacred canopy over your marriage.

Pre-Date Preparation

- Read chapter 9, "Guarding Your Hearts Under God's Canopy."
- Review the Date 9 Exercise (in the back of the book).
- Choose a location that will allow you to talk.

Date-Night Tips

- On this date remember to "pull together."
- Handle tenderly and gently anything your spouse confides in you on this date. There are many resources available for couples whose marriages are touched by pornography, such as www.befreeinchrist.com, which is aimed at men. Another site that offers anonymous help for both the addict and the spouse is www.curethecraving.com.
- Affirm your spouse as he/she shares ways to guard your hearts.

Chapter Summary

Our hearts are important to God and to one another. There are over 950 biblical references to the word *heart*. Most marriages don't fall apart in a day, but rather, couples describe growing apart or slowly turning to someone or something else rather than each other.

Several common temptations can lead our hearts to look away from our spouses. Materialism and accumulation of things that some seek for significance can cause financial stress and tension. Friends at work or social networking sites can become an unhealthy source of companionship. Pornography and lustful images are readily accessible in our culture. These images are like poison in our marriages. Even the obsession for power and success can be destructive to our relationship.

In our culture, we are tempted to look at other marriages, especially those of spiritual leaders, and hold them up as examples to follow. This can lead to disappointment and discouragement when even these marriages fail. God is the author of marriage and the only example of how to love one another that will not fail.

When we commit to live in the safety of God's sacred canopy, we can experience the true joy of a committed marriage that has a divine purpose. Under his canopy, we can connect our faith with our love and our marriage.

Post-Date Spiritual Discovery

Guarding Your Hearts Under God's Canopy

1. Pray—Open with a prayer, asking God to help you protect your marriage by guarding your hearts, using words such as:

   Lord, thank you for your canopy of protection over us. Teach us to seek you each day and guard our hearts from the many temptations that seek to destroy and tear down our marriage.

2. Read—Ephesians 6:10–18

3. Discuss—In this passage, Paul talks about standing firm against evil by putting on God's armor.

   • What are the evil forces and temptations you need to stand firm against in your own life?

   • How are truth, righteousness, peace, faith, salvation, and the Word of God compared to armor?

   • What does Paul say about the role of prayer?

4. Apply—Consider this passage in the context of guarding your heart in marriage.

   • What pieces of God's armor do you want to be more diligent in using to guard your heart?

- Which of these teachings will you practice individually? Which can you observe together as a couple?

5. Close in prayer—Ask God to help you learn to use all the weapons he's given us to guard your hearts and stand firm in his mighty power.

10

Making Your Marriage a Lighthouse

Let your light shine before others, that they may see your good
deeds and glorify your Father in heaven.

Matthew 5:16

Growing up in Minnesota, my (Heather's) family did a lot of
camping and boating. I remember the summer we went on a
boating and camping trip to several islands in Lake Superior.
This huge, cold lake is notorious for its fog and rocks that have
caused many boats and ships to sink.

We were on our second boat propeller of the trip, having already lost one after hitting rocks in the fog. It was our last day,
and we were trying to get home. We tried to follow a ferryboat
for a time, but eventually the fog got too thick to see it. Soon the
fog was so thick we couldn't even see the bow of our own boat.

My dad was using the radio to call for help, while my friend
and I prayed and sang hymns. We were all scared. Finally, after
what felt like hours of staring into the foggy distance, I remember seeing the flashing light of a lighthouse! We knew we were

close to shore. There were still rocks to navigate in the fog, but at last there was hope.

Our marriages can also be a lighthouse to others who are moving through the fog of life. Whether it's your children who are watching you or friends and neighbors who are struggling in their own marriages, your relationship can inspire, comfort, and even provide direction to those around you. There are rocks and fog they will face, but the lighthouse can point them to shore and safety. Your solid marriage can point others to God and give them a sense of hope and direction.

On Date 7, we talked about building our marriage on the firm foundation of God's Word. We looked at the three foundational principles in Genesis 2:24: leaving, cleaving, and becoming one. As we live out God's Word in our daily lives, we can become a lighthouse for other marriages. This, we believe, is God's plan.

Marriage is important to God. Remember, in the beginning God created marriage, and it was very, very good.

> Then God said, "Let us make mankind in our image, in our likeness. . . ." So God created mankind in his own image; in the image of God he created them; male and female he created them.
>
> Genesis 1:26–27

It's a mystery to us, but in a wonderful way, as male and female, husband and wife, we have the potential to reflect God's image to those around us! Our marriage can be a lighthouse to others!

What comes to mind when you think of a lighthouse marriage? We think of:

- Couples who serve each other and those around them.
- Couples who are best friends and have fun together.
- Couples who model commitment, forgiveness, and acceptance.

Service in Marriage

A shared life must have a sacrificial quality, and this leads to service. First we try to serve each other. Then we try to serve others. Have you heard the saying that the first shall be last and the last shall be first? That it's better to give than to receive? Marriages would be revolutionized if we all had a servant's heart.

It's hard to learn to serve each other, especially in the closeness of a marriage relationship, but we (the Arps) quickly learned its importance in developing spiritual intimacy. Dave and I never functioned very well in our marriage when one or the other had to travel. It was especially hard when our children were small and Dave traveled a lot. He would come home exhausted and tired of people. One time stands out in our memory. He was selling data processing services and had worked for months designing a system for a company. This trip was to close the deal. At the last minute, the president of the company reneged. All Dave's hard work was to no avail. He came home empty-handed. No signed contract! He was discouraged and ready to jump into his shell and hibernate.

What was I doing during this time? I was home with a one-year-old and a three-year-old. Our older child had just shared his chicken pox with his baby brother, and I had been homebound and was itching to get out of the house and have some adult conversation. I was ready for reinforcements and couldn't wait for Dave to get home and help!

It didn't exactly work out that way. We were both so caught up in our own miseries that we didn't even think about serving the other. I couldn't understand why Dave couldn't be more sensitive to my needs, and Dave just wanted to be by himself. We exchanged heated words, accusing each other of being selfish.

After being miserable as long as we could stand it, we apologized, and started over again. Years later we still get caught up in the web of "my needs and your needs." We still have to

159

apologize and start over. Knowing the principle doesn't mean we always apply it. But it is our goal to do so.

Think of ways you can serve each other—like being sensitive to your spouse's mood. If I had not crowded Dave when he came home discouraged from that business trip, things could have gone differently. Dave, before getting into his shell, could have gone the extra mile and gone out with me for a couple of hours, or just offered to watch the kids so I could have a breather.

Second, we are committed to serving others. When we acknowledge that our life together is part of the divine purpose, we look for ways to live that out in service to others. Can you think of ways that you can serve others together? Maybe you are concerned about ecology and taking better care of our world. Or perhaps you would like to help an organization like Habitat for Humanity build houses for people who need a place to live. Your own place of worship offers many opportunities for service. Those who desire to serve don't have to look very far to find those who desperately need help! Every time we get involved in serving others together, our own marriage seems to benefit.

What are your areas of strength? How can you use these areas to serve those around you? God has blessed me (Heather) with the gift of hospitality. I enjoy cooking and hosting others in our home. When our children were small, church was a place where I could focus on God and get a short break from parenting our three small ones. Many times I was invited to consider volunteering in the children's programs, but spending more time taking care of more kids would have been a drain for me. The majority of the children's volunteers in our church were college students, and I found that I could serve them and the church by inviting the volunteers to our house for a home-cooked meal. The volunteers enjoyed a break from college food, and our children loved being able to spend extra time with these generous adults.

Fun and Friendship in Marriage

When we think of what attracts us to other couples, we also think of couples who are best friends and really enjoy being together. We all cherish friendships, but there is something special about a husband and wife who are best friends and truly enjoy being together and having fun together. Remember, "Fun in marriage is serious business!" Think about it: Have you ever met a couple on the way to the divorce court who were best friends and having fun together? We don't think so! You can know all the biblical passages on marriage, but if you're not having fun together and enjoying each other, you won't reflect God's image and be a lighthouse to other marriages.

As you are growing together in your faith, take time to have fun, play, and celebrate your marriage. Keep on dating. Let these Great Dates jump-start a habit that will continue through the years. We would encourage you, like Peter and Heather, to adopt a weekly date night. You may not make it happen every week, but by having a designated time, you will be able to make dating a priority in your marriage. If you are looking for dating suggestions, start by reviewing the suggestions in Date 5. You can also check out several other resources listed in the front of the book.

Besides a regular date night, other practical ways to have fun together might include investing in a shared interest or activity. If you are having a hard time coming up with ideas for joint activities, go out on a brainstorming date and make a long list of the things you like and the things you would like to try together. When we (the Larsons) were living in California, we were fortunate enough to know a couple in their eighties who were still fostering new interests and a great friendship. On one occasion, Peter was helping the couple set up for a party. When asked about the event, the couple explained they were hosting a party for all the students in the art history class they were taking at the local community college together. We are never too old to learn new things or try new activities together.

Over the years our marriage (the Arps') has been enriched by our ability to foster a positive, playful, and enjoyable relationship. Fun, humor, and celebration are like vitamins for the soul. They are also good for your marriage's health, and for the health of your children as well.

We asked our friend Howard, who has been married more than fifty years and has a great marriage, what he remembered about his parents. What did they pass on to him that made his relationship with his wife so special? He thought for a moment and said,

> There are two things that stand out. At first they didn't seem to be related, but the more I think about it, they really are. First, I remember my parents praying together. Whatever hard situations we were facing in our family, we prayed about it. The second thing I remember is hearing my parents roaring with laughter. They enjoyed each other, and they made life fun for all of us.

An enriched, fun-loving marriage can make a difference in your quality of life while impacting your family for generations to come. We can leave the heritage of a truly enriched, spiritually intimate marriage to others, including our children, grandchildren, and their spouses.

Commitment in Marriage

Do you model commitment in your marriage daily? You might be surprised that others are watching. We (the Larsons) mentioned how we've tried to serve others by hosting the volunteer youth leaders from our church for dinner. Heather's hospitality always sets the stage for a great evening. Inviting others into our home, even for a meal, gives them a glimpse into the way things function in our marriage. We've been told on more than one occasion that our marriage (and parenting) were powerful examples to the young men and women who were our dinner guests. It is not uncommon to hear these young people report how they grew up in homes with dysfunctional models of what a marriage could be. Many of these dinner guests have become close friends who have seen our marriage as a lighthouse for their own marriages.

Commitment in marriage is more than hanging on during the good times. It is also being committed when the road is rough and hard. Scott Stanley, in his book *The Heart of Commitment*, talks about two kinds of marital commitment. One, the commitment of dedication, should be part of every marriage. That's the commitment we demonstrate when all is going well and we are "so in love" and just can't stand to be apart. Every marriage needs this kind of commitment to survive, but it's unrealistic to assume that you will have it all the time.

A second kind of commitment is also needed: the commitment of constraint. That's the commitment you need when things aren't going so well. It's the kind of commitment that says, "I don't like you very much right now, but I'm totally committed to you, and I'm not going anywhere—and if you leave me, I'm going with you!" In a healthy lighthouse marriage, you need both the commitment of dedication and the commitment of constraint. Remember, no one has the dedication kind of commitment 24/7.

If you are in a hard place in your relationship, let us encourage you. Things can and will get better if you're committed to going the distance together. In one national survey of households and families, sociologist and researcher Linda Waite did a follow-up study with married couples who had described themselves as "unhappy" five years earlier. Of those who stayed married, 86 percent reported their marriages had become happier. Research has shown there are seasons in a marriage, with natural ups and downs. Transitions such as moves, births, changing jobs, retiring, or embracing the empty-nest years will all cause fluctuations in marriage satisfaction. But for those couples who stay committed to going the distance, they find the good outweighs the bad, and they learn they can count on one another in all seasons of their marriage.[1]

One couple, Bill and Ann, had been married for thirty-five years. Together, they managed to raise three children and save for retirement, but something was lacking—they had not felt connected in several years. They had never learned to communicate well, so when things were tense, they tended to criticize each other, argue, and eventually pull away. Bill invested more time in his job, where he felt successful and respected. Ann put her energies into raising the kids, volunteering, and running the household. This seemed to work until their youngest child moved out and Bill began to contemplate retirement. *Was it time for a divorce?* They were like strangers living under the same roof.

Instead, with the wise counsel of their pastor, they decided to work on reconnecting. They began to travel, read, and even attended some marriage enrichment seminars. For the first time in years, they began to really communicate and rediscover those things that first attracted them to each other. In the end, they were thankful they persevered. Their only regret was not working on their relationship earlier.

Your Marriage—a Lighthouse

Your marriage can be a lighthouse to a hurting and confused world. Are you willing to take the torch and pass the message on to others of how to have an enriched, healthy marriage? Today we need a widespread movement that will produce large numbers of marriages that provide working models of committed and creative love in human relationships, and you can be part of this movement.

We hope we have inspired you to want to be a lighthouse to other marriages and that you will choose to reach out together in your church, neighborhood, and/or community. Your marriage can be that lighthouse. You can be a catalyst for lighting thousands of lights—you'll never know how many others your life will influence by making your marriage a lighthouse. Your marriage can make an eternal difference in the lives of others.

If you light one log in the fireplace by itself, the flame may go dim, but several logs together burn brightly. To keep the fires of your marriage burning brightly, consider organizing a Great Dates group through your church or community, or you may want to simply invite a few other couples into your home. Challenge them to join with you. Commit yourselves to each other to be encouragers to keep on building truly enriched, alive marriages. You could use this book as your guide or Great Dates Connect or the 10 Great Dates to Energize Your Marriage DVD video-based program.

You'll find the dating approach is an easy-to-lead, inviting, and encouraging approach for couples. Even the one who is typically the "dragee" will participate. After all, how much trouble can you get in on a date? Plus, you will find that it really helps to have supportive friends who gently nudge you to grow your marriage.

How does a 10 Great Dates group work? It's very simple: Get together with other couples for about thirty to forty-five minutes for your date launch. Our leader's guide (at www.10greatdates .org) makes it simple to facilitate great discussions and help couples connect with other couples. Your church is an ideal place to offer dates to help couples grow together spiritually. And couples will come. Think about it: If you are the church on the corner that offers child care and fun dates, couples will come!

A lighthouse marriage is strong, secure, and, at times, a place of refuge. Is your marriage strong and secure? Then share it with others. A lighthouse guides boats in fog or in a storm. Are there hurting couples you can reach out to and mentor? Lighthouses must be maintained constantly. Are you continually making your marriage a priority? Then help others do the same!

What will your children and others around you remember about your marriage? Will they see unconditional love, forgiveness, and acceptance reflected in your love for each other? Will they observe you serving each other and others? Will they see you living out your wedding vows daily as you go through both the good times and the not-so-good times with a lifelong commitment? Will your marriage inspire them to work hard at having an alive, spiritually intimate marriage? Will they remember laughter and celebration? Do they see you making your marriage a priority? These are great questions to talk about on this date!

Now it's time to turn the page to Date 10 in the Dating Guide, set goals for the future, and enjoy celebrating your spiritual journey and your love.

Great Date 10

Making Your Marriage a Lighthouse

On this date you'll enjoy celebrating your spiritual journey and talking about how your marriage can be a lighthouse to other couples.

Pre-Date Preparation

- Read chapter 10, "Making Your Marriage a Lighthouse."
- Fill out the Date 10 Exercise (in the back of the book).

Date-Night Tips

- Be willing to work together to formulate goals for your marriage.
- Be realistic and choose goals that are achievable.
- If you know something your spouse really wants to do together, give a gift of love and agree to do it!

Chapter Summary

Just like a lighthouse in the fog, a solid marriage can point others to God and give them a sense of hope and direction. Being created in God's image, we have the potential of reflecting God's image to those around us. A lighthouse marriage is one that has a posture of service. We can serve one another in our marriage and put the needs of our spouse ahead of our own. In our self-focused society, we can also share God's love through the sacrifice of serving others.

Being a lighthouse is not all work. It's a lot of fun too. Laughter is contagious, and keeping the joy in your marriage is an encouragement to those around you. To keep the fun in your marriage, remember to keep dating each other, focus on the positive, and take time to be each other's friend.

Similar to a physically solid lighthouse, our marriage must have a strong foundation. The foundation in marriage is commitment. Commit to one another that your marriage is for a lifetime. Relationships that are committed will need forgiveness and acceptance. Share your lighthouse marriage with those around you.

Post-Date Spiritual Discovery

Making Your Marriage a Lighthouse

1. Pray—Open with a prayer, thanking God for leading you on this spiritual journey together:

   Lord, we thank you for the opportunity to explore our spiritual journey as a couple. Thank you for giving us the courage to connect on such an intimate level. We ask that you continue to lead us as a spiritually connected couple in the months and years ahead, tuning our hearts and minds to your will for our lives.

2. Read—Psalm 20:4 and 2 Timothy 4:7

3. Discuss—God desires your marriage to be successful. He is committed to you and to your marriage.

   • What are the desires of your heart for your marriage?

   • What goals have you set for your marriage?

   • Paul speaks of his accomplishments and of finishing the race. What do you want your marriage to look like at the finish line?

   • What must you fight for and fight against to maintain a loving and growing Christian marriage?

- In what ways are you willing to let the Lord make your marriage a lighthouse of hope and direction for others?

4. Apply—Pray with one another this week that God will continue to transform your relationship into a lighthouse marriage. Discuss ways your marriage can be an example to your family, friends, and neighbors.

5. Close in prayer—Thank God for meeting you on this journey and pray that he'll continue to lead in your lives individually and as a couple. Pray for wisdom, protection, and guidance.

Acknowledgments

We are deeply indebted to everyone who contributed to this project . . .

All the couples who have participated in our 10 Great Dates programs and seminars who have encouraged us to address the important topic of connecting faith and marriage.

Dianne Weakley, the Arps' personal angel, who keeps us sane and skillfully handles all the myriad details for Marriage Alive.

Our spiritual journeys have been blessed by a number of special people who have walked before us, alongside us, and behind us. Many have been mentors, small-group members, family, and friends. Our gratitude for your encouragement and thoughtfulness is immeasurable.

Notes

Date 1: Connecting Faith and Love

1. David Olson and Peter Larson, PREPARE/ENRICH Program, Customized Version, (Minneapolis: Life Innovations, 2008).

2. Quote found at www.goodreads.com/author/quotes/319733.Tertullian.

Date 2: Appreciating Your Differences

1. David Olson, Amy Olson-Sigg, and Peter Larson, ENRICH Inventory (Minneapolis: Life Innovations, 2008).

2. David and Claudia Arp, *The Second Half of Marriage* (Grand Rapids, MI: Zondervan, 1996), 58–59.

3. Daniel Amen, *Change Your Brain, Change Your Life* (New York: Time Books, 1998), 64–67.

4. Jane Kise, David Stark, and Sandra Krebs Hirsh, *Lifekeys: Discover Who You Are* (Bloomington, MN: Bethany House, 2005).

Date 3: Experiencing God Together

1. Gary Thomas, *Sacred Pathways* (Grand Rapids, MI: Zondervan, 2000), 21–22.

2. Les and Leslie Parrott, *Saving Your Marriage Before It Starts* (Grand Rapids, MI: Zondervan, 1995), 135.

3. David Olson, Amy Olson-Sigg, and Peter Larson, PREPARE/ENRICH Inventory (Minneapolis: Life Innovations, 2008).

4. Drs. Les and Leslie Parrott, *Saving Your Marriage Before It Starts,* 145.

Date 5: Loving Your Closest Neighbor

1. David Olson, Amy Olson-Sigg, and Peter Larson, PREPARE/ENRICH Inventory (Minneapolis: Life Innovations, 2008).

2. John Gottman, *Why Marriages Succeed or Fail* (New York: Simon & Schuster, 1994), 29.

Notes

Date 6: Talking Together With God

1. David and Jan Stoop, *The Complete Marriage Book* (Grand Rapids, MI: Revell, 2002), 310.
2. Ibid., 308–309.
3. David and Claudia Arp, *The Second Half of Marriage* (Grand Rapids, MI: Zondervan, 1996), 182.
4. Stoop, *The Complete Marriage Book,* 309.
5. Mark Butler, et al., "Prayer as a Conflict Resolution Ritual," *The American Journal of Family Therapy*, 30, no. 1 (2002): 19–37; and "Not Just a Time-Out," *Family Process*, 37, no. 4(2004): 451–478.

Date 7: Building Your Marriage on a Strong Foundation

1. Olson, Olson-Sigg, and Larson, PREPARE/ENRICH Inventory.
2. Robert Sternberg, "A Triangular Theory of Love," *Psychological Review*, 93 (1986): 119–135.
3. Olson, Olson-Sigg, and Larson, PREPARE/ENRICH Inventory.

Date 9: Guarding Your Hearts Under God's Canopy

1. Catherine Rampell, "Money Fights Predict Divorce Rates," *New York Times*, December 7, 2009, accessed at http://economix.blogs.nytimes.com/2009/12/07/money-fights-predict-divorce-rates/.
2. Jerry Ropelato, compiler, "Internet Pornography Statistics," accessed at http://internet-filter-review.toptenreviews.com/internet-pornography-statistics-pg4.html.
3. Rachel Duke, "More Women Lured to Pornography Addiction," *Washington Times*, July 11, 2010, accessed at http://www.washingtontimes.com/news/2010/jul/11/more-women-lured-to-pornography-addiction/.
4. Lydia Saad, "Cultural Tolerance for Divorce Grows to 70%" May 19, 2008, accessed at http://www.gallup.com/poll/107380/cultural-tolerance-divorce-grows-70.aspx.
5. Bono, as quoted by David Yonke, "Leadership Seminar Reaches 80,000," *Toledo Blade*, August 12, 2006, in a story about an interview Bono did with Bill Hybels, pastor of Willow Creek Church: www.toledoblade.com/Religion/2006/08/12/Leadership-seminar-reaches-80-000.html.
6. Stephen Post, *Spheres of Love* (Dallas: Southern Methodist Press, 1994), 18–19.
7. Ibid.
8. David and Vera Mace, *What's Happening in Clergy Marriages?* (Nashville: Abingdon, 1980), 100–103.

Date 10: Making Your Marriage a Lighthouse

1. Linda Waite and Maggie Gallagher, *The Case for Marriage* (New York: Doubleday, 2000), 148.

Claudia Arp and David Arp, MSW, are founders of Marriage Alive International, a groundbreaking ministry dedicated to providing resources and training to empower churches to help build better marriages. The Arps are authors of numerous books and video curricula, including the 10 Great Dates series and the Gold Medallion Award–winning *The Second Half of Marriage*. Frequent contributors to print and broadcast media, the Arps have appeared on the NBC *Today Show*, CBS *This Morning*, and *Focus on the Family*. Their work has been featured in publications such as *USA Today*, the *Washington Post*, *New York Times*, *Wall Street Journal*, and *Time* magazine.

Peter J. Larson, PhD, is a licensed clinical psychologist and former president of Life Innovations, the international headquarters for PREPARE/ENRICH. He is the coauthor of the PREPARE/ENRICH Customized Version and the Couple Checkup Inventory and book. Heather Larson, MS, has her master's degree in psychology. She is the founder of Bridgewell Coaching and works as a Christian life coach. She and Peter regularly teach and speak together. They are the hosts of the 10 Great Dates Before You Say "I Do" DVD curriculum. The Larsons have been married for almost twenty years and have three children.

GREAT DATE 1 EXERCISE

Connecting Faith and Love

On this date, we want you to take a trip down your "Faith Journey Memory Lane" and share your memories with each other. *(Note: For this exercise and the others, duplicate copies are provided for you and your spouse.)*

Your Family Experience

Describe the religious atmosphere in your home growing up.

Was a belief in God important in your family?

What religious practices took place at home?

Who took responsibility for them?

How did spiritual beliefs affect decisions and behavior in your family?

In what ways were they meaningful or not meaningful to you?

Your Church Experience

Did your family attend church?

If you attended church during your childhood, what was it like?

Were you ever involved in a youth group? If so, what was your experience?

Your Personal Experience

1. Where are you on your spiritual journey today?

    ___ Committed   ___ Seeking

    ___ Returning   ___ On fire

    ___ Lukewarm   ___ Resistant

    ___ Growing   ___ Other: _____

2. What events or experiences (positive or negative) in your life have had special meaning to you?

3. Who has most influenced you in your faith?

Your Couple Experience

1. How important is the spiritual dimension in your relationship?

2. What is one hope or desire you have for your spiritual life together?

Connecting Faith and Love

On this date, we want you to take a trip down your "Faith Journey Memory Lane" and share your memories with each other.

Your Family Experience

Describe the religious atmosphere in your home growing up.

Was a belief in God important in your family?

What religious practices took place at home?

Who took responsibility for them?

How did spiritual beliefs affect decisions and behavior in your family?

In what way were they meaningful or not meaningful to you?

Your Church Experience

Did your family attend church?

If you attended church during your childhood, what was it like?

Were you ever involved in a youth group? If so, what was your experience?

Your Personal Experience

1. Where are you on your spiritual journey today?
   ___ Committed   ___ Seeking
   ___ Returning   ___ On fire
   ___ Lukewarm   ___ Resistant
   ___ Growing   ___ Other: _____

2. What events or experiences (positive or negative) in your life have had special meaning to you?

3. Who has most influenced you in your faith?

Your Couple Experience

1. How important is the spiritual dimension in your relationship?

2. What is one hope or desire you have for your spiritual life together?

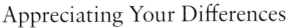

Appreciating Your Differences

Identifying and Accepting Differences

1. Consider the following categories and talk about the ways in which you are different.
   - Family background/traditions/cultural differences
   - Personality
   - Gender differences
   - Interests/hobbies

2. How do your differences bring balance to your relationship?

3. How do your strengths benefit your marriage and family?

4. How can you do a better job of honoring and accepting each other's differences?

_____

_____

_____

_____

Identifying Your Spiritual Gifts

As you consider growing together spiritually, think about how your spiritual gifts have an impact on your relationship.

What are your spiritual interests and gifts? (See a short list of gifts in the Post-Date Spiritual Discovery at the end of chapter 2.)

How do your different spiritual gifts play out in your relationship and spiritual lives?

In what ways are you similar?

Are there areas where you typically "clash" or experience tension?

How do your spiritual gifts complement each other?

Appreciating Your Differences

Identifying and Accepting Differences

1. Consider the following categories and talk about the ways in which you are different.
   - Family background/traditions/cultural differences
   - Personality
   - Gender differences
   - Interests/hobbies

2. How do your differences bring balance to your relationship?

3. How do your strengths benefit your marriage and family?

4. How can you do a better job of honoring and accepting each other's differences?

_____

_____

_____

_____

Identifying Your Spiritual Gifts

As you consider growing together spiritually, think about how your spiritual gifts have an impact on your relationship.

What are your spiritual interests and gifts? (See a short list of gifts in the Post-Date Spiritual Discovery at the end of chapter 2.)

How do your different spiritual gifts play out in your relationship and spiritual lives?

In what ways are you similar?

Are there areas where you typically "clash" or experience tension?

How do your spiritual gifts complement each other?

Experiencing God Together

Taking a Spiritual Experience Survey

Consider the following pathways of spiritual experience. On a scale of 1 to 5 (5 being very effective and 1 being not so effective), rate how each facet helps you experience God. Now rate them as you think your spouse would rate them. Compare your lists and discuss.

You Your spouse
___ ___ Attending church and hearing a good sermon
___ ___ Worship through singing of hymns
___ ___ Worship through singing modern praise songs
___ ___ Small-group study
___ ___ Sunday school class
___ ___ Personal devotions/quiet time
___ ___ Giving to the church and other charities
___ ___ Forgiving each other
___ ___ Celebrating religious holidays
___ ___ Reading the Bible together
___ ___ Having devotions together
___ ___ Praying together
___ ___ Serving others together
___ ___ Experiencing nature together
___ ___ Sharing a creative activity (gardening, cooking, etc.)

In what ways are you alike or different?

What surprises you about each of your rankings?

_____

_____

_____

_____

Discussion Questions

1. What are the fundamental values that you and your spouse share?

_____

_____

_____

_____

2. What are your core spiritual beliefs? Consider the following areas:
   • Marriage
   • Finances
   • Family
   • Parenting
   • Work/service

3. How does your experience of God relate to your values and core beliefs?

Experiencing God Together

Taking a Spiritual Experience Survey

Consider the following pathways of spiritual experience. On a scale of 1 to 5 (5 being very effective and 1 being not so effective), rate how each facet helps you experience God. Now rate them as you think your spouse would rate them. Compare your lists and discuss.

You Your spouse
___ ___ Attending church and hearing a good sermon
___ ___ Worship through singing of hymns
___ ___ Worship through singing modern praise songs
___ ___ Small-group study
___ ___ Sunday school class
___ ___ Personal devotions/quiet time
___ ___ Giving to the church and other charities
___ ___ Forgiving each other
___ ___ Celebrating religious holidays
___ ___ Reading the Bible together
___ ___ Having devotions together
___ ___ Praying together
___ ___ Serving others together
___ ___ Experiencing nature together
___ ___ Sharing a creative activity (gardening, cooking, etc.)

In what ways are you alike or different?

What surprises you about each of your rankings?

_____

_____

_____

_____

Discussion Questions

1. What are the fundamental values that you and your spouse share?

_____

_____

_____

2. What are your core spiritual beliefs? Consider the following areas:
   - Marriage
   - Finances
   - Family
   - Parenting
   - Work/service

3. How does your experience of God relate to your values and core beliefs?

Getting Into the Word

Discuss the following:

What has been your experience reading the Bible?

Which books, passages, or verses of the Bible are the most meaningful to you? Why?

_____

_____

_____

_____

_____

_____

In thinking about getting into the Word together, which do you find most appealing?

_____ Join or start a Bible study group

_____ Participate in an ongoing small-group study

_____ Participate in a book study

_____ Do a couple's devotional book or other resource together

_____ Watch DVDs or listen to podcasts

_____ Read online devotions

_____ Listen to online sermons

_____ Read the Bible in a year

_____ Download a Bible app for your smartphone

_____ Have a daily quiet time

What are your plans for getting into the Word?

As an individual?

As a couple?

Reflect and Review

Consider how your previous times of spiritual discovery have gone:

1. Have you been able to find time to complete them as a couple?

2. If so, how has that experience been?

How open are you to making a couple's devotional time part of your weekly routine?

Getting Into the Word

Discuss the following:

What has been your experience reading the Bible?

Which books, passages, or verses of the Bible are the most meaningful to you? Why?

_____

_____

_____

_____

_____

_____

In thinking about getting into the Word together, which do you find most appealing?

_____ Join or start a Bible study group

_____ Participate in an ongoing small-group study

_____ Participate in a book study

_____ Do a couple's devotional book or other resource together

_____ Watch DVDs or listen to podcasts

_____ Read online devotions

_____ Listen to online sermons

_____ Read the Bible in a year

_____ Download a Bible app for your smartphone

_____ Have a daily quiet time

What are your plans for getting into the Word?

As an individual?

As a couple?

Reflect and Review

Consider how your previous times of spiritual discovery have gone:

1. Have you been able to find time to complete them as a couple?

2. If so, how has that experience been?

How open are you to making a couple's devotional time part of your weekly routine?

Loving Your Closest Neighbor

"I Feel Loved When You . . ."

Complete the following sentence in at least five different ways:

I feel loved when you . . .	Write here how your spouse feels loved.
_____	_____
_____	_____
_____	_____
_____	_____
_____	_____
_____	_____

Now take turns sharing your sentences with each other and take notes on what your spouse shares with you.

Caution: Your spouse's list should not be viewed as commands or things you have to do—no guilt intended here. Instead, view them as options and opportunities to show love.

Tip: Try to do at least one thing on your spouse's list this week!

Make a Philippians Treasure-Chest List

> Finally, brothers and sisters, whatever is true, whatever is noble, whatever is right, whatever is pure, whatever is lovely, whatever is admirable—if anything is excellent or praiseworthy—think about such things.
>
> Philippians 4:8

Philippians 4:8 can help us control our attitudes and thoughts and help us look for the positive in our spouse. Think about your spouse's positive qualities and list one under each of the following qualities:

One thing that is true (such as love and commitment)

One thing that is noble (such as honesty and integrity)

One thing that is right (such as investing time in our relationship)

One thing that is pure (such as being faithful)

One thing that is lovely (such as being creative and thoughtful)

One thing that is admirable (such as volunteering to help others)

One thing that is praiseworthy (such as helping a stranger)

Take turns sharing your lists with each other and celebrate the positive!

Loving Your Closest Neighbor

"I Feel Loved When You . . ."

Complete the following sentence in at least five different ways:

I feel loved when you . . .	Write here how your spouse feels loved.
_____	_____
_____	_____
_____	_____
_____	_____
_____	_____

Now take turns sharing your sentences with each other and take notes on what your spouse shares with you.

Caution: Your spouse's list should not be viewed as commands or things you have to do—no guilt intended here. Instead, view them as options and opportunities to show love.

Tip: Try to do at least one thing on your spouse's list this week!

Make a Philippians Treasure-Chest List

Finally, brothers and sisters, whatever is true, whatever is noble, whatever is right, whatever is pure, whatever is lovely, whatever is admirable—if anything is excellent or praiseworthy—think about such things.

Philippians 4:8

Philippians 4:8 can help us control our attitudes and thoughts and help us look for the positive in our spouse. Think about your spouse's positive qualities and list one under each of the following qualities:

One thing that is true (such as love and commitment)

One thing that is noble (such as honesty and integrity)

One thing that is right (such as investing time in our relationship)

One thing that is pure (such as being faithful)

One thing that is lovely (such as being creative and thoughtful)

One thing that is admirable (such as volunteering to help others)

One thing that is praiseworthy (such as helping a stranger)

Take turns sharing your lists with each other and celebrate the positive!

Talking Together With God

Looking Back

In thinking about your life, in what ways do you see God's hand?

_____

_____

_____

_____

_____

Can you think of ways God has answered prayers in the past?

_____

_____

_____

_____

_____

What about a time when God said no and it turned out for your good?

_____

_____

_____

_____

_____

Looking Ahead

Make a prayer list together as you consider the following topics:

What I would like you to pray for me:

What I would like to pray for you:

What I would like to pray for us:

Prayer requests for others:

Experiencing Prayer Together

Pray through your lists together. Agree on an approach to prayer in which you both feel comfortable, such as taking turns, making a list, or praying silently together.

Talking Together With God

Looking Back

In thinking about your life, in what ways do you see God's hand?

_____

_____

_____

_____

_____

Can you think of ways God has answered prayers in the past?

_____

_____

_____

_____

_____

What about a time when God said no and it turned out for your good?

_____

_____

_____

_____

_____

Looking Ahead

Make a prayer list together as you consider the following topics:

What I would like you to pray for me:

What I would like to pray for you:

What I would like to pray for us:

Prayer requests for others:

Experiencing Prayer Together

Pray through your lists together. Agree on an approach to prayer in which you both feel comfortable, such as taking turns, making a list, or praying silently together.

Building Your Marriage on a Strong Foundation

Consider the following three foundational principles and evaluate your own relationship. Place yourself on each continuum with 1 being very low and 10 being very high:

Leave—Commitment: "For this cause a man shall leave his mother and father . . ."

Low	1	2	3	4	5	6	7	8	9	10	High

Circle where you would place yourself on this continuum, then place an X where you see your spouse.

1. Can you think of a time when you put your spouse before your parents, or brothers or sisters?

   your children?

   your career?

   your hobbies and/or other activities?

2. What adjustments might you need to make? Is there something you need to leave or make a lower priority in order to make your spouse a higher priority?

Cleave—Intimacy: "And cleave to his wife . . ."

Low	1	2	3	4	5	6	7	8	9	10	High

Circle where you would place yourself on this continuum, then place an X where you see your spouse.

1. How do you presently express your commitment to cleave to each other?

2. What tends to pull you together?

3. What tends to push you apart?

4. Make a list of things you can do together that would help you to cleave to each other.

5. Make a list of things you want to avoid doing that tend to put distance in your relationship.

Become One—Passion: "And they will become one flesh."

Low	1	2	3	4	5	6	7	8	9	10	High

Circle where you would place yourself on this continuum, then place an X where you see your spouse.

1. What are some ways you could add passion to your love life? (more hugs, more kisses, more tender touches?)

2. Do you need to schedule more time for loving each other?

Tip: Passion, like faith, often comes when we step out and take the risk. If you have children and don't plan, passion probably won't happen on its own.

Building Your Marriage on a Strong Foundation

Consider the following three foundational principles and evaluate your own relationship. Place yourself on each continuum with 1 being very low and 10 being very high:

Leave—Commitment: "For this cause a man shall leave his mother and father . . ."

Low	1	2	3	4	5	6	7	8	9	10	High

Circle where you would place yourself on this continuum, then place an X where you see your spouse.

   1. Can you think of a time when you put your spouse before your parents, or brothers or sisters?

      your children?

      your career?

      your hobbies and/or other activities?

   2. What adjustments might you need to make? Is there something you need to leave or make a lower priority in order to make your spouse a higher priority?

Cleave—Intimacy: "And cleave to his wife . . ."

Low	1	2	3	4	5	6	7	8	9	10	High

Circle where you would place yourself on this continuum, then place an X where you see your spouse.

1. How do you presently express your commitment to cleave to each other?

2. What tends to pull you together?

3. What tends to push you apart?

4. Make a list of things you can do together that would help you to cleave to each other.

5. Make a list of things you want to avoid doing that tend to put distance in your relationship.

Become One—Passion: "And they will become one flesh."

Low	1	2	3	4	5	6	7	8	9	10	High

Circle where you would place yourself on this continuum, then place an X where you see your spouse.

1. What are some ways you could add passion to your love life? (more hugs, more kisses, more tender touches?)

2. Do you need to schedule more time for loving each other?

Tip: Passion, like faith, often comes when we step out and take the risk. If you have children and don't plan, passion probably won't happen on its own.

Facing the Storms
of Life Together

What major storms have you faced in your life and marriage?
Use this list as a memory jogger:

Job changes

Moves

Family stress

Health issues

Financial needs

Relationships

Think of different situations or passages in life that tend to
be stressful. How did God meet your needs in those situations?

Identify One Storm You've Faced Together

Tip: You might *not* want to choose the most major or a very
emotional storm to talk about on this date.

Discuss the following:

- How did you face this storm? (Attacked it head-on? Ignored it and hoped it would go away? Worked on facing
  it together?)

- Do storms tend to draw you closer to God and/or to each other? In what ways?

- What did you learn about yourself, your relationship, and God through this storm?

- Sometimes, looking back, it's easier to see a storm more clearly, having a better perspective. Can you see now how God was with you during that time?

Consider Future Storms

This side of heaven, we can always count on there being future storms. How can you prepare yourself spiritually to face the future storms of life?

Tip: Consider behaviors (such as studying the Bible) as well as attitudes (such as embracing realistic expectations) that will be helpful to you in preparing for life's storms.

Facing the Storms of Life Together

What major storms have you faced in your life and marriage? Use this list as a memory jogger:

Job changes

Moves

Family stress

Health issues

Financial needs

Relationships

Think of different situations or passages in life that tend to be stressful. How did God meet your needs in those situations?

Identify One Storm You've Faced Together

Tip: You might *not* want to choose the most major or a very emotional storm to talk about on this date.

Discuss the following:

- How did you face this storm? (Attacked it head-on? Ignored it and hoped it would go away? Worked on facing it together?)

- Do storms tend to draw you closer to God and/or to each other? In what ways?

- What did you learn about yourself, your relationship, and God through this storm?

- Sometimes, looking back, it's easier to see a storm more clearly, having a better perspective. Can you see now how God was with you during that time?

Consider Future Storms

This side of heaven, we can always count on there being future storms. How can you prepare yourself spiritually to face the future storms of life?

Tip: Consider behaviors (such as studying the Bible) as well as attitudes (such as embracing realistic expectations) that will be helpful to you in preparing for life's storms.

Guarding Your Hearts Under God's Canopy

Think about some temptations. Which ones are the most problematic for you? (materialism, busyness, success and achievement, pornography, infidelity, pride, arrogance, and so on).

1. Consider your list above and talk about how you are guarding your own heart against some of these temptations.

2. Talk about how you can ensure that God's canopy is over your marriage. Consider and discuss the following practical suggestions. Which ones do you relate to?

   Praying together

   Reading the Bible

   Seeking a closer, loving relationship with God

   Joining a small group

   Finding a mentor or accountability partner

   Going to counseling

   Reading helpful books

   Changing your computer habits

   Changing your television viewing habits

   Setting new boundaries at work or at home

Other

_____

_____

_____

_____

Guarding Your Hearts Under God's Canopy

Think about some temptations. Which ones are the most problematic for you? (materialism, busyness, success and achievement, pornography, infidelity, pride, arrogance, and so on).

1. Consider your list above and talk about how you are guarding your own heart against some of these temptations.

2. Talk about how you can ensure that God's canopy is over your marriage. Consider and discuss the following practical suggestions. Which ones do you relate to?

   Praying together

   Reading the Bible

   Seeking a closer, loving relationship with God

   Joining a small group

   Finding a mentor or accountability partner

   Going to counseling

   Reading helpful books

   Changing your computer habits

   Changing your television viewing habits

   Setting new boundaries at work or at home

Other

_____

_____

_____

_____

Making Your Marriage a Lighthouse

Sharing New Insights

Look back over the last nine dates and talk about new insights you have gained.

    1. What changes have you made?

    2. What are your areas of strength?

    3. What growth areas would you like to work on together?

Setting Goals for the Future

To help you develop a deeper spiritual connection and relationship with each other, choose one or two of the following goals to concentrate on, or use the list as a catalyst to come up with your own goals.

    1. To develop more common interests and get to know my spouse better. To really cleave!

    2. To remember life is not all about work. Have fun together!

    3. To strengthen our commitment to our marriage and to each other.

4. To improve communication with one another and to learn to express myself in a better way (including talking about spiritual topics).

5. To become more creative in our sexual relationship, adding passion with God's blessing!

6. To become more united and responsible in our finances and in our giving to others in need.

7. To learn to better process anger and talk through issues in a loving and positive way.

8. To choose a project to do together or a service project for someone else.

9. To deepen our spiritual intimacy by starting a regular prayer and devotional time together.

Your Marriage—a Mission

We suggest writing out your own Marriage Mission Statement. You can make it as simple or as elaborate as you want to. The key is that you both agree on your final statement. One couple who had several small children came up with a very simple mission statement: Survive and abide!

Making Your Marriage a Lighthouse

Sharing New Insights

Look back over the last nine dates and talk about new insights you have gained.

1. What changes have you made?

2. What are your areas of strength?

3. What growth areas would you like to work on together?

Setting Goals for the Future

To help you develop a deeper spiritual connection and relationship with each other, choose one or two of the following goals to concentrate on, or use the list as a catalyst to come up with your own goals.

1. To develop more common interests and get to know my spouse better. To really cleave!

2. To remember life is not all about work. Have fun together!

3. To strengthen our commitment to our marriage and to each other.

4. To improve communication with one another and to learn to express myself in a better way (including talking about spiritual topics).

5. To become more creative in our sexual relationship, adding passion with God's blessing!

6. To become more united and responsible in our finances and in our giving to others in need.

7. To learn to better process anger and talk through issues in a loving and positive way.

8. To choose a project to do together or a service project for someone else.

9. To deepen our spiritual intimacy by starting a regular prayer and devotional time together.

Your Marriage—a Mission

We suggest writing out your own Marriage Mission Statement. You can make it as simple or as elaborate as you want to. The key is that you both agree on your final statement. One couple who had several small children came up with a very simple mission statement: Survive and abide!